THE WAY OF
THE ENGLISH MYSTICS

An Antho

THE WAY OF
THE ENGLISH MYSTICS

An Anthology and Guide for Pilgrims

Gordon L. Miller

BURNS & OATES

First published 1996
BURNS & OATES,
Wellwood, North Farm Road,
Tunbridge Wells, Kent TN2 3DR

ISBN 0 86012 209 3

Line drawings and maps by Penelope Burns

*The picture on the front cover, showing the disciples on the road
to Emmaus, in the guise of medieval pilgrims, is taken from the
fourteenth-century* Bible de Sens.

Burns & Oates publish books of general Christian interest including
lives of the saints, prayer, spirituality and mysticism, church history,
doctrine and life, theology, philosophy, Bible reading.

A free catalogue will be sent on request:
BURNS & OATES, Dept A,
Wellwood, North Farm Road,
Tunbridge Wells, Kent TN2 3DR
Tel: (01892) 510850   Fax: (01892) 515903

Typeset by Search Press Ltd
Printed and bound in Great Britain by
Biddles Ltd, Guildford and King's Lynn

CONTENTS

ACKNOWLEDGEMENTS

I should like to convey my gratitude to the people who have helped in the long development of this book. My wife, Jacquelyn, offered encouragement and assistance from the beginning. Paul Burns, besides making most of the versions of the extracts from the medieval mystics used in this book, provided sustained interest and editorial advice, as well as historical and geographical additions to the text. Denise Thompson and Tom Slaughter supplied valuable suggestions on the Introduction. And Orvel Crowder, to whom the book is dedicated, stimulated my interest many years ago in the Christian mystical tradition and, through inspired teaching, preaching, and personal example, helped me to understand its meaning and relevance for twentieth-century spiritual life.

The publishers would like to thank the Friends of Julian of Norwich, the Friends of St Margaret's, King's Lynn, and Mr and Mrs Grove of Hall Farm, King's Cliffe, for providing material for the relevant illustrations.

To Orvel Crowder,
who pointed the way

INTRODUCTION

Few things are more urgently and universally needed today than the cultivation of a sense of the sacred. Faced with divisions and disharmonies both within and without, we need to discover a way of living that promotes healing, a way of being that is based not on the existence and perpetuation of the parts of reality but is informed by the wisdom of the whole. For wholeness is of the essence of the holy, the sacred.

We sense the subtle intimation of the sacred whenever something or someone touches us deeply and becomes for us something more, a living symbol of an encompassing and ultimate reality. When we feel the rhythms of our bodies—the beating of our hearts, the movement of our breath—as part of the larger pulse or rhythm of nature, we are approaching a sense of the sacred. When the vastness of the ocean or the silent immensity of the mountains speaks to us of a transcendent presence, we are in sacred communion. When religious rituals, art, and architecture ignite a spark of mystery in us, the sacred is shining through. When, in the midst of our inner monologue or outer dialogue, we are startled by a glimpse of full human contact, or when the caring and acceptance of friends or family gives us a feeling of belonging, of being at home, of being whole, the sacred is at hand. When, whatever the circumstances, we are spoken to, whispered to, from a deeper dimension, and know that to live from that dimension would be to live in a different world, the sacred is speaking to us, inviting us. How can we attune ourselves more fully, so that we can hear and respond wholeheartedly to this healing voice?

The development and promotion of the perspective of the whole is implied in the meaning of the term religion—"to bind back." In their best and truest forms, the religions of humanity have served this unifying function. In most of these religious traditions, including early and biblical Christianity, the idea of salvation has universal, cosmic dimensions. Thus it is not only the individual soul that is seen as in need of salvation; the entire world—body, mind, nature, and society—needs to be healed, harmonized, and made whole. The theologian Paul Tillich, in discussing the identity between salvation and healing in the history of religious thought, points out that "when salvation has cosmic significance, healing is not only included in it, but salvation can be described as the act of 'cosmic healing'." He says, further, that the decisive sign of such salvation is reconciliation, the re-establishment of a lost unity within oneself, with others, with nature, and with God, and that "reconciliation in the center of personality results in a reconciliation in all directions, and he who is reconciled is able to love. Salvation is the healing of the cosmic disease which prevents love."[1] Salvation in this sense thus involves a resanctifying or re-enchantment of the world.

We must remember, of course, that many ardent religious adherents have often contributed not to the harmony and integration of life but, rather, to the discord between mind and body, between person and person, and even between individuals and God. Devotees sometimes perpetuate fragmentation through exclusive attachment to the partial and imperfect expressions of ultimate reality enshrined in their particular symbols, concepts, doctrines, and texts. Symbols, however, lose their life and force when they cease to be vital signs of the sacred and become enclosed within the sphere of the self, when they become merely aspects of the structure and activity of the rational mind. A religion limited to this realm loses its cosmic implications and stops short of any true sense of the sacred. A life limited to this realm—to the voices and visions of the mind, which are always selective and partial—is doomed to discord and dissatisfaction. This is life out of balance, an imbalance that manifests itself in all manner of physical, psychological, social, and ecological disorders.

This imbalance has been the concern of innumerable spiritual masters, both Eastern and Western, who proclaim the necessity and the sanity of going beyond the self, of going, on a daily basis, "out of one's mind." The teachings of these spiritual masters are designed to redress the imbalance that afflicts human nature, so that the dry fields of thought will be irrigated by a deeper Reason, and the shrill voice of logic will resonate with the spirit of the *Logos*, the cosmic Word. The mystical aspect of religion involves going beyond religious ideas and experiencing the realities to which they refer. But mysticism is not only a way of going to the heart of religion, it is a way of going to the heart of life, to the heart of oneself—from knowledge to wisdom, from emotionality to deep feeling, from compulsive cogitation and verbalization to yearnings too deep for words. As the Benedictine monk John Main has said, through the practice of meditative prayer "you will eventually be unhooked from your ideas, your concepts, your words, your thoughts, all that amalgam of distraction that is going on in your mind most of the time, and you will come, with patience and with fidelity, to clarity of consciousness."[2] Such a practice is a way of going from fragmentation to wholeness, for "when the perfect comes, the partial will be done away" (1 Cor. 13:10). The mind then becomes not a purveyor of partiality, but, rather, an energized instrument of integration.

The revival of interest in various forms of meditation and mysticism in recent decades, both among those inside and those outside the fold of traditional Western religion, is evidence that many people are searching for a deeper level of meaning or experience, for a more authentic and integrated way of feeling their existence. One of the beneficial side effects of the importation of Eastern forms of spirituality has been the rediscovery of the rich tradition of mysticism within Christianity. In the Christian mystical tradition, many people have found the meditative spirit and methods so evident in Eastern religions, but couched in a symbolism and a religious heritage with which they can much more readily identify. Participants in this tradition speak of Incarnation, Crucifixion, and Resurrection, of redemption from sin and love for one another, of Father, Son, and Holy Spirit, of Matthew, Mark, Luke, and John.

But they also provide a larger perspective by emphasizing that the heart of religion lies not in the holding of particular concepts or creeds, but, instead, in the manifestation of the sacred in one's life. The idea is to go from a belief in the Word becoming flesh to the experience of this process in one's own body and mind; from entertaining the idea of resurrection to actually enjoying newness of life; from considering the future possibility of eternal life to feeling one's present existence from a timeless perspective, an "eternal now." Mysticism appeals to those who feel the need for a religion that genuinely transforms one's being, that harmonizes the body, transfigures perception, shifts the tenor of one's thought, and activates a healing energy and intelligence in the world. The Christian mystical tradition proposes a way of listening to the *Logos* that not only informs, but also in-forms, and that allows the Word to resound in the depths of one's being, to form sentences, paragraphs, a life story.

The Christian mystics represented in this book speak to us from different eras of the religious life of England, and they convey a variety of its aspects. Five of them—Richard Rolle, Walter Hilton, the anonymous author of *The Cloud of Unknowing*, Julian of Norwich, and Margery Kempe—are drawn from the medieval period, specifically the fourteenth and fifteenth centuries, the era that could be considered the golden age of English mysticism. George Herbert and William Law represent a later, more secular age—the seventeenth and eighteenth centuries—though their devotional standards and practices were certainly no less rigorous than those of their predecessors. All of these writers, with differing emphases and distinctive forms of speech, convey the message that we exist in the embrace of a mystery, a divine mystery touching us at the very center of ourselves, of which we are but dimly aware. They develop the themes of humility, of inner detachment, of love and service to others, and of meditative prayer as aspects of the spiritual life, as ways of realizing and responding to the mysterious touch.

These writers also emphasize, in one way or another, that the spiritual life is a process, a pilgrimage. Like the measured advance of the dawn, the illumination of mind and body is not accomplished in an instant; Incarnation is a process of continuous creation and evolution. In *The Scale of Perfection*, Walter Hilton says that a soul "cannot suddenly jump from the lowest to the highest, any more than a man who will climb a high ladder and puts his foot on the lowest rung can at the next moment be on the top one. He must go up them in order until he comes to the highest."[3] In making this ascent the key is not concern with one's advancement but, rather, the clarification of one's intention and the cultivation of one's availability. I can set my feet to the ladder, but I cannot raise them from rung to rung. The most I can do is to situate myself on the ladder in a posture of least resistance, so that the ascent can be effected in me as easily and as gracefully as possible.

To engage in this inner pilgrimage requires no outer excursions at all. However, throughout the ages innumerable spiritual pilgrims have undertaken geographical pilgrimages as well. The motivations for these journeys are, no doubt, many and varied; some hope for healing, some desire visions, some, perhaps, search for perspective. But all such pilgrims, it seems, seek to participate in something larger than themselves—in the common spirit of fellow pilgrims, or in the universal Spirit that is their deepest stimulus and ultimate goal. Millions have travelled annually to Mecca, to Lourdes, or to Canterbury, and in recent decades many Westerners have journeyed to the East in search of the sacred. We flock to those places where a larger measure of mystery has appeared, and perhaps remains, in the hope that this outer orientation of ourselves in time and space will facilitate an inner reformation.

The spirit of pilgrimage has always been close to the heart of mysticism, not only in the sense that pilgrims seek an immediate experience of ultimate reality, but also because pursuing a physical pilgrimage is in accord with the mystical sentiment that ideas and abstractions alone are not enough, that true spirituality seeks a deeper engagement with concrete realities. Meditative prayer is a way of cultivating such engagement; pilgrimage can also be a way.

Pursuing a particular pilgrimage can also strengthen the pilgrim's involvement with his or her religious tradition. It is with this possibility in mind that this book provides information on the lives and locations of each of these Christian mystics, as well as details of their historical contexts and spiritual heritage. Many people have discovered the wisdom of these spiritual masters in recent years through the increased availability of their writings. The selections included in this book reflect the major themes of each of the writers, and will, it is hoped, serve as an incentive to readers to seek out the larger works from which they have been drawn. But it is also hoped that the book as a whole will encourage you, the reader, to visit the sites from which these writings arose. Visiting the haunts of the English mystics can help one to situate their ageless message in time and place, and can strengthen one's awareness of, and sense of identification with, this rich Christian tradition, a tradition devoted to strengthening our sense of the sacred. This sensitivity permeated the lives of the English mystics represented here as they, in their monasteries and sanctuaries from the rolling hills of the Midlands to the ancient villages of East Anglia, carried out their devotions and provided spiritual direction.

Simon Tugwell, in commenting on the spirituality of *The Cloud of Unknowing*, has said that "the contemplative does not 'see God'; he enters into God's seeing."[4] The essence of pilgrimage, whether inner or outer, is not, strictly speaking, the seeking of a certain kind of spiritual experience; it is, rather, the pursuit and practice of living from a deeper dimension. In cultivating a sense of the sacred, the essential and perennial human task is the preparation of a fertile inner field of stillness and spaciousness, so that the holy can take hold and bear fruit.

Notes

1. Paul Tillich, *The Meaning of Health: Essays in Existentialism, Psychoanalysis, and Religion*, edited by Perry LeFevre (Chicago: Exploration Press, 1984), pp. 17, 21.

2. John Main, *The Inner Christ* (London: Darton, Longman & Todd, 1987), p. 191.

3. Walter Hilton, *The Scale of Perfection*, trans. into Modern English, with an Introduction and Notes, by Dom Gerard Sitwell (London: Burns & Oates, 1953), p. 183.

4. Simon Tugwell, "Preface" to *The Cloud of Unknowing*, edited and with an Introduction by James Walsh (New York: Paulist Press, 1981), p. xxii.

Richard Rolle

*Plaque commemorating Richard Rolle at Hampole,
near the site of the former Hampole Priory*

RICHARD ROLLE

In a chapel in Yorkshire around the middle of the fourteenth century, a solitary hermit sitting in meditation was surprised by the igniting of an intense but pleasant bodily heat. He repeatedly touched his chest, thinking that his rising temperature might have had some physical cause. But finding none, he determined that this phenomenon was a spiritual manifestation, a realization that fuelled his delight. Commenting on the lighting of this inner flame, Richard Rolle says that "before the infusion of this comfort I had never thought that we exiles could possibly have known such warmth, so sweet was the devotion it kindled. It set my soul aglow as if a real fire was burning there."[1]

When one considers the national upheavals and international conflicts, the darkening shadows of disease and death, and the ecclesiastical divisions that surrounded Rolle in his chapel, it seems that perhaps never has the guidance of an inner light been more needed for finding one's way through the darkness. England was embroiled with France in the Hundred Years' War from 1337 to 1453 and the effects were being felt throughout English society. The bubonic plague, or Black Death, struck in 1348-9, killing at least a third of the population and, with the resulting rise in the value of the surviving labourers, led to the Peasants' Revolt of 1381, which signalled a growing spirit of democracy and the gradual break-up of medieval feudalism.

Perhaps of more immediate concern to the English mystics were the disruptions within the Church. The question of papal authority was being contested by both religious and secular leaders, with the tensions issuing first in the so-called Babylonian Captivity and then in the Great Schism between the Eastern and Western Churches. In the face of such religious turmoil, the spiritual life of the people, though nourished by many popular and entertaining miracle plays performed in churchyard and marketplace, was in need of direction from true spiritual masters. Evelyn Underhill notes that "in vivid contrast to the state of the official Church . . . was the network of mystical devotion—mostly propagated by groups of lay-folk gathered round some saintly character—which had spread over Western Europe and attracted to itself all fervent spirits."[2] Richard Rolle was probably the first and most familiar of these "saintly characters" in England, and through his teaching and writing he initiated something of a fourteenth-century spiritual revival.

The particulars of Rolle's life are relatively plentiful compared with most of the other English mystics of his day, thanks both to his own writings and to a document called the *Legenda*, which was compiled by the nuns at Hampole Priory in anticipation of his canonization as a saint.[3] Details of his birth and childhood are, nevertheless, quite few, but he apparently was born around the year 1300 in the village of Thornton-le-Dale, near Pickering, in North Yorkshire. He entered the University of Oxford at about the age of fourteen, being sponsored there by Thomas Neville, one-time archdeacon of Durham. His studies over five or six years were evidently marked by good progress, as he acquired the foundations of scholarship, encountered the subtle distinctions of philosophical thought and the agonistic drama of theological debate, and was perhaps especially drawn to the sermons and simple spirituality of the Franciscan friars, who were very influential in Oxford at that time. But he left the university rather suddenly at the age of nineteen, without receiving a degree, and returned home to Thornton.

Upon arriving back in Yorkshire, Rolle wasted no time in strengthening his commitment to the spiritual life, a desire that perhaps hastened his exit from Oxford, by running away from home to become a hermit. The *Legenda* contains the story of his constructing a makeshift hermit's outfit from a rain hood of his father's and two of his sister's dresses, whereupon his beloved sister exclaimed: "My brother is mad! My brother is mad!" Fearing a similar diagnosis by other family members and friends, he went to a nearby church, perhaps at Malton or Pickering, to pray. He was there recognized by the sons of a local squire named John de Dalton as having been with them at Oxford. The next day he preached a moving sermon in the church, whereupon the squire, being a friend of Rolle's father and having become convinced of the young man's sincerity both through this public demonstration and through a subsequent private conversation, took it upon himself to provide him with the proper clothing and the necessary food and private place within his home for Rolle to pursue his vocation.

It appears that Rolle stayed for an extended period with the Daltons before moving on to other hermitages, mixing solitary spirituality with community services, and perhaps stayed from time to time in the friaries of the Augustinian hermits, though he never established any particular institutional engagement. In pursuing this way of life he was in quite good and plentiful company in fourteenth-century Yorkshire, where about one hundred hermits or anchorites lived, often attached to one of the fourteen abbeys, ten priories, or thirty friaries.

Later in life he came to reside in the village of Hampole, northwest of Doncaster, where he served as spiritual director to the nuns of a Cistercian convent and to an anchoress named Margaret Kirkby. Rolle most likely lived in a solitary cell in a wooded area near the nunnery, whose chapel probably served as the local church. The nunnery was founded around 1170 and by the first half of the fourteenth century was evidently in dire need of moral and spiritual guidance. Many Yorkshire nunneries during this period were small and poor and were constantly threatened by raiding armies from England and Scotland. This vulnerability and poverty seemed to contribute to a state of moral laxity and lack of discipline, and one historian has commented that, indeed, "there were no more quarrelsome nunneries in the kingdom."[4] Over a period of years following Rolle's death on 30 September 1349 (he was possibly a victim of the plague), the Hampole nuns worked to make a case for his canonization by preparing the *Legenda*, thus recording selected episodes of his life and providing accounts of a number of miraculous healings associated with him or with pilgrimages to his tomb. Though his sainthood was never formally recognized by the Church, he was venerated as such by many people for some two hundred years, up to the eve of the Reformation.

The nunnery was evidently located on the bank of a small stream and sustained the life of the community until well into the sixteenth century. Today nothing remains of the nunnery as such, though pieces of the carved stonework were apparently built into some of the surrounding structures and churches in the area. Rolle's cell and tomb have also disappeared. But marking the site of his hermitage is a small stone monument with a plaque describing him as a "Mystic, Evangelist, Spiritual Guide and Author of many religious writings including 'The Fire of Love' written here in 1343."

Rolle, who was commonly known as the "Hermit of Hampole," was one of the most popular and prolific religious writers of the fourteenth century. He wrote scriptural commentaries, psalters, long treatises, short essays, and poems, which together contain vivid imagery, autobiographical passages, and numerous borrowings from great works in the tradition of Christian spirituality, including those of St Augustine, St Bernard, St Bonaventure, and Richard of St Victor. While many of his works, including *The Fire of Love*, were in Latin, he was one of the earliest writers to express himself in English. His pioneering translations of scripture were utilized by John Wycliffe in the preparation of the English Bible and he has even been considered by some to be the "father of English literature." He thus played an important role in bringing the Bible and other religious writings to a wider range of readers, including women and laypeople, beyond the professional clergy and educated aristocracy.

Rolle's writings are marked by emotional intensity and indeed the most distinctive feature of *The Fire of Love*, his best-known work, is its blending of spirituality and physicality. Rolle assures us that the warmth he felt, which occurred only after nearly four years of solitary discipline and devotion, was real, sensible, not imaginary, heat. He also speaks of hearing a symphony of spiritual sounds that resonated in his mind so that, as he describes it in Chapter Fifteen, "my thinking itself turned into melodious song, and my meditation became a poem." With his body warmed and his ordinary mental prose transformed into an inner poetry, Rolle found that a wonderful sweetness pervaded his being and deepened his amazement that experiences such as these were afforded to mere mortals.

Though the inclusion of the body within the life of the spirit is more evident in non-Christian than in Christian thought, sensuous displays such as Rolle's warmth, sound, and sweetness, are accepted, and even expected, elements of spiritual practice in the Eastern Orthodox tradition. Clifton Wolters points out that Orthodox Christian mystics understand that "prayer affects the whole person, and spiritual emotions do sometimes express themselves in bodily feelings. It is Western Christians who are over-cerebralized in their approach to things of the Spirit, and who need to be reminded of this simple truth."[5] Rolle, indeed, can help remind us that spiritual development is not separate from the material, biological, and mental realms, but is, rather, a universal process occurring in a perhaps unsuspected dimension within these realms.

Rolle's style of spirituality, especially his fondness for singing, the simplicity and intimacy of his expressions, and his attention to concrete manifestations of the divine, bears significant similarities to that of St Francis of Assisi in the previous century. It is also, it seems, at least with regard to his sense of the burning immediacy of the divine presence, particularly consonant with the sentiment expressed by a twentieth-century Christian mystic. Pierre Teilhard de Chardin, with characteristic faith in the future, has written that "the day will come when, after harnessing [space], the winds, the tides, gravitation, we shall harness for God the energies of love. And, on that day, for the second time in the history of the world, man will have discovered fire."[6] As Richard Rolle found, that discovery often awaits the fervent pilgrim with an openness to the gracious uplift of the Spirit.

The site of the former Hampole Priory is just off the A638 main road, about six miles north-west of Doncaster and a mile from the intersection with the A1, in the West Riding (from a Scandinavian word for "third") section of Yorkshire, now officially just "West

21

Yorkshire." Much of the road from Doncaster to Hampole forms part of the route traditionally known as the Great North Road. This historic highway followed, for most of its length, the ancient Roman road called Ermine Street, leading from London through Lincoln, York, and northward. In Yorkshire it was built on a narrow belt of magnesian limestone that, when the Romans arrived, formed the only strip of firm, dry ground through the marshy land. For centuries its noisy traffic shaped the settlements along its route, as it brought soldiers, peddlers, princes, hermits, and pilgrims to this area long known for its coalfields, sheep farms, woollen mills, and monasteries.

This is also the land of Robin Hood. About a mile north of Hampole, just to the west of the A1 near Skelbrooke, is Robin Hood's Well, where the legendary hero is said to have made the Bishop of Hereford dance in his boots. It has even been suggested that Richard Rolle, known for his lyrical writing, might have composed some of the well-known ballads of this mythical figure and his merry men.[7]

Notes

1. Richard Rolle, *The Fire of Love*, trans. and with an Introduction by Clifton Wolters (Harmondsworth: Penguin Books, 1972), p. 45. Of the extracts that follow, that from *The Fire of Love* is in a version made specially for this book; *The Love of God* and *Contemplation* are taken from J. Griffiths, (ed.), *The Cell of Self-knowledge* (Dublin: Gill and Macmillan; New York: Crossroad, 1981).

2. Evelyn Underhill, *The Mystics of the Church* (Cambridge: James Clarke, 1925. Reprint. Wilton, Conn.: Morehouse-Barlow, 1988), p. 153.

3. See Frances M. M. Comper's *The Life of Richard Rolle* (London: J. M. Dent, 1929. Reprint. New York: Barnes and Noble, 1969) for a thorough account of Rolle's life in relation to his times, a collection of his poetry, and a translation of the *Legenda*.

4. Eileen Power, *Medieval English Nunneries* (Cambridge: Cambridge University Press, 1929), p. 597.

5. Clifton Wolters, "The English Mystics," in *The Study of Spirituality*, edited by Cheslyn Jones, Geoffrey Wainwright, and Edward Yarnold (Oxford and New York: Oxford University Press, 1986), p. 332

6. Pierre Teilhard de Chardin, *Toward the Future*, trans. René Hague (New York: Harcourt Brace Jovanovich, 1975), pp. 86-7.

7. See Hope Emily Allen, *Writings Ascribed to Richard Rolle, Hermit of Hampole, and Materials for His Biography* (New York: D. C. Heath, 1927), p. 511 note 3.

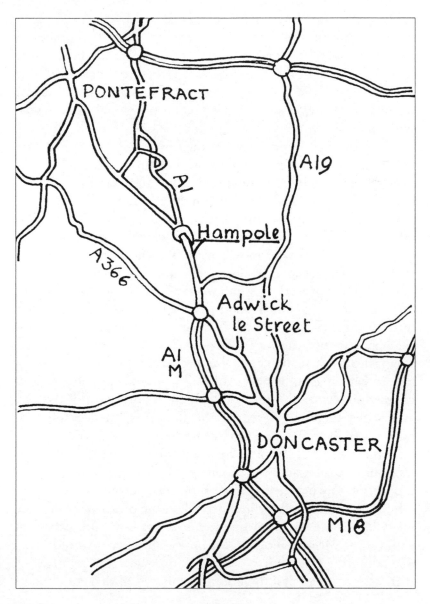

THE FIRE OF DIVINE LOVE

PROLOGUE

I was more astonished than I can say when, for the first time, I felt my heart glow hot and burn. I experienced the burning not in my imagination, but in reality, as if it were being done by a physical fire. But I was really amazed by the way the burning heat boiled up in my soul and (because I had never before experienced this abundance), by the unprecedented comfort it brought. In fact, I frequently felt my chest to see if this burning might have some external cause!

But when I had recognized that the fire of love had boiled over not from the flesh with its concupiscence (in which I continued to dwell), but solely from the spirit within, and that it was the gift of the Creator, I melted, rejoicing, in the experience of a love even more intense. This melting happened chiefly because of the influence of the love and the sweetness which, with the spiritual heat itself, inwardly and most pleasantly penetrated my spirit to the very marrow. Indeed, before that comforting heat was poured into me, flooding every devotion with sweetness, I had not thought such ardour could come inwardly to anyone in this exile here on earth, for it inflamed my soul in such a way that it was just as if elemental fire burned there.

This fire is not at all like the fire that inflames others burning in love of Christ, as some have said it is, seeing people carrying out divine duties with diligence and contempt of the world. But just as when a finger is placed in the fire it experiences physical burning, so the soul set on fire by love in the way I have described feels the most real burning desire. Sometimes that burning is lesser in intensity, and sometimes greater; when it is less, it is in proportion to what the fragility of the flesh permits.

Indeed, who could bear in mortal flesh the presence of that fire for a long time in its most intense degree—to the extent of enduring it without interruption in this life? This would make one fail in the face of that sweetness and before the greatness of that feeling heated past the boiling point and of that inestimable burning; without a doubt it would be embraced with avidity and when one had been made glorious with these gifts of the spirit, one would desire with the most ardent sighs that, breathing forth one's soul in this honey-sweet fire itself, one might stay there, departing from the world and immediately being held captive among the community of those singing praises to the Creator.

Certain things, though, opposed to charity, get in the way because the filths of the flesh take one by surprise and disturb one's tranquillity. In addition, the needs of the body, intense human affections and the difficulties of living in this world break in upon one, and change the shape of this burning love and lessen and disturb the "flame." (I have called this love "fire" as a metaphor, because it burns and illumines.) These things certainly do not steal what cannot be taken away because this wraps up the entire heart. Then that most blessed glowing fervour, absent till then on account of such things, appears. I remain as if frozen until it returns to me, and feel abandoned while I do not have (as I have been accustomed to) that sense of inner fire to which my whole body and spirit give praise and in which they know themselves secure.

Besides these things, sleep gets in my way like an enemy, because the only time I must mourn as lost is that which I am forced to surrender to sleeping. In fact, keeping vigil, I try to warm my soul, made dark by the cold as it were; I have known it, undisturbed in devotion, to be set on fire, and to be raised by enormous desire indisputably above earth-dwellers.

For the fullness of eternal love has not come to me in idleness, nor have I been able to feel that spiritual burning desire while I have been physically much fatigued on account of travel, nor, again, while occupied immoderately by the comforts of the world, nor even while given over, beyond reason, to theological debates. On the contrary, I have found myself growing cold in such activities until, having laid aside all those things by which I could be detained outside, I once again struggled to place myself exclusively in the presence of the Saviour, and once again stayed with the ardours burning within me.

Therefore, I offer this book for consideration not by philosophers, not by the worldly-wise, not by great theologians ensnared in endless questionings, but by the unsophisticated and the untaught, who are trying to love God rather than to know many things. For God is known in doing and in loving, not in arguing.

Moreover, I observe that those things that are considered by these questioners (who are superior to everyone else in knowledge, but are inferior in the love of Christ), cannot be understood. For this reason I have decided not to write for these people, unless, having put aside and forgotten all those things that have to do with the world, they burn to be enslaved by single-minded desires for the Creator.

First, however, in order that they may flee all earthly rank, they must hate all the ostentation and empty glory of learning; then, conforming themselves most strictly to poverty, they must continually place themselves in the love of God by praying and meditating. In this way, without a doubt, a certain small interior flame of uncreated love will appear to them and, focussing their hearts on grasping this fire (by which all darkness is consumed), will raise them up in lovable and most pleasing burning ardour. In this way, they will transcend earthly things and cling to the throne of tranquillity forever. Indeed, because these people are more learned, they may, by that fact, be better adapted for loving, if they truly despise themselves and rejoice to be rejected by others.

Accordingly, because I am rousing everyone here to love, and because I will try to show the superheated and supernatural feeling of love to everyone, the title *The Fire of Love* is chosen for this book.

CHAPTER FIFTEEN

In what manner and for how long a time the writer has been drawn to the solitary life; the joyous song of love; concerning the changing of dwelling places

When I was growing up unhappily, with a wary adolescence upon me, the grace of the Creator poured forth. God restrained my longings for temporal beauty and turned me to desiring non-bodily embraces. Raising my soul from the depths, God carried it over to the heavens so that I might burn especially for the delight of eternity, more fully than I ever delighted before in the embraces of the flesh and the joys of the world.

So much so, that if I wanted to show how favourable the outcome has been, I should have to praise the solitary life, since the Spirit breathed on me and bent my intention toward following and loving this life, which I then took care to lead, to the extent that my weaknesses allowed me. Nevertheless, I have stayed among people who have flourished in the ways of the world, accepting food from them, and hearing such flatteries as would drag celebrated warriors down from the heights to the depths. But by casting away things of this kind for the sake of the One, my soul has been lifted up to the love of the Author, and in my desire to delight in eternal sweetness, I have made over my soul to love God with the devotion He accepts especially from his beloved, in order to make the most delightful solitude visible to my soul and to teach it to count as nothing the sustaining comforts that come from men's erroneous ways.

In fact, I have been used to seeking quiet, however much I used to travel from one place to another. It is not wicked for hermits to leave their cells for good reason and to return to them again when it seems suitable to do so. Indeed, several of the holy Desert Fathers did so, despite the murmuring from people (but not from the good ones) they thus attracted. Evil folk spoke evil of them because that was their way: they would have done the same had the hermits remained in their cells. When you lift the lid of the latrine, nothing comes out but a stink! Those who speak evil do so from a heart filled with vipers' venom.

I know this from my own experience: the more I have strived to make spiritual progress, the more I have been calumnied with detracting words. And the worst of my detractors are those I formerly thought my truest friends. But I have not stopped doing what is useful to my soul on account of their words. On the contrary, I have followed my desire, and I have always found God befriending me. I have recalled the words of scripture, "They shall speak evil and you shall bless" (Ps. 108:28). And as time has passed, I have been granted progress in spiritual joys.

From the time I first altered my way of life and spirit, to when the door of heaven opened to me (allowing the eye of my heart to contemplate heavenly beings with their beauty revealed, to see the road leading to its Beloved and to sigh continually for Him), took three years, all but three or four months. Then the door remained open for almost a further year before I really felt the heat of eternal love in my heart. In fact, I was sitting in a particular chapel, greatly delighting in the smooth flow of my prayer or meditation, when I suddenly experienced within myself an unaccustomed and joyous burning ardour. Although I first doubted where this might be coming from, I have since proved, over a long period of time, that it comes not from any creature but from the Creator, since it is more burning and more agreeable. Then, from when that inestimably delightful heat first blazed in my senses to the infusion and perception of the celestial or spiritual sound that belongs to the hymn of eternal praise and the smoothness of invisible melody (which cannot be known or heard except by those who receive it—and they must be cleansed or separated from the earth),* nine months and several weeks elapsed.

I was then sitting in that same chapel, singing the Psalms in the evening before supper, as well as I was able. Suddenly, the sound of, as it were, the ringing, or rather playing of stringed instruments, above me, made me jump. Then, when I strained toward these heavenly sounds by praying with all my heart, I experienced—I do not know how soon—the blending of melodies within myself and drew forth the most delightful harmony from heaven, which stayed with me, in my spirit. My meditation was continually transformed into the song of harmony, as if I had odes in meditating. Furthermore, I have since enjoyed that same sound in psalmody and in the prayers themselves. Then I have hastened into the presence of this flowing forth of inward, indeed hidden, sweetness, to the singing I have described, because I have

---

*Referred to as the divine harmony or "song of angels" by Walter Hilton: see below, pp. 58-63.

thus been hastening into the presence of my Creator alone. . . .

Meanwhile, I was seized with wonder at being raised into such great joy while in exile here, and because God had given me gifts such as I did not know how to ask for—indeed, I could not think that even the holiest person in the world could receive such gifts in this life. This leads me to think that such a gift is not given to anyone in recompense for merit, but gratuitously, to whomever Christ wills it. Nevertheless, I canot think that it would be granted to anyone who did not love the name of Jesus especially, and honour it so much as never to allow it to fade from memory, except in sleep. My view is that those to whom the gift of doing this has been given will reach this state.

From the beginning of my change of soul to the final degree of love of Christ that I had the God-given strength to attain—the stage at which divine praises resounded in me with the melody of jubilant song—took a further four years and some three months.

This state, in those disposed to it by previous experience, will certainly last to the end of their lives. And it will become even more perfect after death, since the joy of love, this fire of charity, has been kindled and will receive its most glorious consummation in the kingdom of heaven. Those who are embarked on these steps in this life will profit not a little, but will not ascend into another state; they will rest (as mortals can) as though confirmed in grace.

So I desire to give praises and thanks without ceasing back to God, who has comforted me in my anxieties and vexations, and caused me to seek an eternal crown with confidence, amid prosperities and flatteries, saying:

From this place, O Jesus, I continually give praises to you, who have deigned to become one with me, the most wretched and least of men, but sending out my small measure of melody from my spirit (but from heaven) as one of your melody-making ministers. I shall take care to give thanks with joy, since you have enabled me to fashion myself excellently to the singing, through a clear conscience in a soul burning with eternal love, loving and boiling, sitting in fire. My spirit is transformed, burning with heat and ardently dilated with desire. Its true beauty of delightful virtue blooms without a blemish in the sight of the Creator; jubilant song pours forth when the Creator gives joy to the languishing soul with joyful singing and lessens its burdens.

There are many great and wonderful rewards, but none to compare with these, which so preciously strengthen hope by implanting a kind of invisible life in the loving soul, or which so delightfully console us where we are and snatch us up to the peak of contemplation, or to the harmony of angelic praise.

So, my brothers and sisters, I have told you how I have attained the fire of love, not so that you will praise me, but so that you will glorify my God, from whom I have received whatever blessing I have, and so that you, judging everything under the sun as vanity, may be encouraged to imitate me, not decry me.

THE LOVE OF GOD

Sweet light, joyous light, you the unmade who made me, enlighten the contours and working of my inward eye with unmade clarity. Shine into my mind so that it is wholly cleansed and so exalted by your gifts that it rushes into the full happiness of love. Kindle it with your sweet fire so that I may sit in you, Jesus, and rest there full of joy, walking about as if ravished by heavenly sweetness and always beholding unseen things. Let me be glad in God alone.

Everlasting love, inflame my soul until I love God so much that nothing burns in me but his desires. Good Jesus, no one but you can help me so to feel you that I feel no one and nothing but you, and see no one and nothing but you. Shed yourself into the innermost depths of my soul. Come into my heart and fill it with your clearest sweetness. Moisten my mind with your sweet love's hot wine so that I forget all unhappiness and all ridiculous dreams. Let me be happy only in your presence in me and rejoice only in Jesus, my God. From now on, sweetest Lord, do not leave me. Stay with me wholeheartedly in all your sweetness, for my only comfort is your presence and only your absence can make me sorrowful.

Holy Spirit, you give grace wherever you wish. Come into me and ravish me until I am yours. Use your honey-sweet gifts to change the nature that you made, so that I am fulfilled in your loving joy and my soul despises and throws away everything in this world. Burn my longing so that my heart glows for ever on your altar. Sweet and true joy, come to me, I pray you. Come, sweet and most desired love. Come to me my love; come to me my comfort; come!

Use your sweet heat to urge longing for you from my soul. Kindle the whole of my heart with your love. With your light enlighten my inward being. Feed me with the honey-song of your love. May my soul find gladness in this and similar meditations and get to the very pith of love. Love truly suffers and assails the lover, not so that a loving soul should stay wrapped up in itself, but so that the soul is more where it loves than where the body is that lives and feels that love.

There are three degrees of Christ's love into which, one after the other, anyone is called who is chosen to love. The first is "unable to be overcome." The second is "unable to be parted." The third is "singular," or "oned."

Love is truly unable to be overcome when it cannot be overcome by any other desire. It cannot be overcome when the lover first throws off all hindrances and all temptations and destroys all physical desires, and then patiently suffers all unhappiness for Christ's sake, and cannot be overcome by any flattery or any inclination. To a lover all labour is light. The best way to overcome difficulties is to love.

Love truly cannot be parted when the mind is fired with great love, and draws close to Christ with all thoughts concentrated on him. Indeed, it can't allow him out of mind for even a second, but, as if imprisoned in heart, it sighs to him and cries out to be clasped to him by his love and to throw off mortal bonds, begging him to do nothing but lead it to what it desires. The lover worships and loves the name "Jesus" so much that it is the constant preoccupation of the mind. And so, when the heart of Christ is in the heart of God's lover, and the world is despised so much that no other desire of love can overcome it, it is called "high." But when he or she holds fast to Christ, undeparted from Christ, always thinking of Christ, never forgetting Christ for any reason whatsoever, it is called "everlasting" and "undeparted."

But what can happen to this love which is "high" and "everlasting"?

Well, there is the third degree, which is called "singular." It is one thing to be "high," and another to be "oned" to Christ. It is one thing to have Christ always present in one, and another to have no other companion but Christ. We may have a great crowd of companions and still reserve the first place for Christ. If you really look for some other comfort and get something from someone or something other than your God, and if you happen to love whatever it is, then your love is not "singular." You can see then how very great an achievement it is if you move on from the stage of being "high" to that of being alone or "oned." Love ascends to this "singular" degree when it shuts out all comforts but the comfort it finds in Jesus, and when nothing but Jesus will satisfy it.

In this third degree the soul is intent on loving Christ alone. It yearns for Christ alone and desires no one but Christ. It lives only in his desire, sighs only to him, burns only in him, and rests only in his warmth. It finds nothing else sweet and nothing else tasty. It becomes sweet only in Jesus, in whose mind all is music and song and feasting with wine. It doesn't matter what the self thinks up for itself and happens on, it will soon be cast down if it does not serve Jesus' desire and follow his will.

Whatever the self does seems pointless and intolerable unless it pushes and leads desire toward Christ.

When the soul loves Christ it believes it has all it can ever want to have. Without Christ all things become vexing and noisome. But whoever truly loves Jesus endlessly and steadfastly lives in his body, and does not become weary in heart but loves perseveringly and suffers everything gladly. The more that anyone lives like this in Christ, the more love is kindled, and the more it becomes like Jesus himself. The more the soul is ravished to the point of joy, the less it is occupied by outward things, and the less it is filled with the cares and burdens of this life. Thus a soul that at the start couldn't stand even the least pain is held back by no anguish whatsoever, for it finds its joy in God always and ever.

Soul, stop loving this world. Melt in the love of Christ. Put everything else aside and discover how sweet it is to speak of him, to read of him, to write of him, to think of him, to pray to him and praise him always. God, my soul is devoted to you and longs to see you. It cries out to you from a long way off. It burns in you. It yearns in your love and in love of you. Love that never fails, you have overcome me. Everlasting sweetness, everlasting beauty, you have wounded my heart. I am so overcome and wounded by you that I fall. I am so full of joy and I can scarcely go on living. I almost die. This perishable flesh cannot stand such great sweetness, such vast majesty. All my heart is truly bound up in the love of Jesus; it becomes the white heat of love, to be swallowed into another form. Therefore, good Jesus, have mercy on this wretched creature. Show yourself to my longing self. Heal me in my sickness. Anyone who does not love you loses everything. Anyone who does not follow you is mad. So always be my joy, my love and my desire, so that I may see you in Sion, God of gods.

Charity is truly the noblest of the virtues. It is the best and sweetest of things that Jesus should be loved by the lover and that Christ should be everlastingly joined in the chosen soul. Such love remakes the image of the Trinity in us; it makes human creatures most like him who made them.

The gift of love is of more value than all other gifts, for it rivals even the high degree of angels. The more truly we in this life share in love, the greater and higher in heaven we shall be. Joy of everlasting love, you are unique, for you turn all our longings and desires toward the heavens above all worlds, fixing them there with bonds of virtue. Without charity no one can really do anything worthwhile, whatever else he or she may have.

Anyone who is truly possessed by the spirit of charity is raised up into a joy above this world, and enters boldly the bed-chamber of the everlasting King. Do not be ashamed to take no one but Christ, for it is Christ whom you have sought and loved. Christ is yours. Hold fast to him, so that he who is the only one you wish to obey holds fast to you. Charity, you are sweet and consoling. You make whole what was broken, you free captives, you raise us up to the condition of angels. Sitting and resting, you raise us up and, when raised up, we are made sweet by you.

Love in this degree or state is chaste and holy. It is concerned altogether with what is loved. There is nothing outward-looking that can please it. It lives in the soul, sweet-smelling and whole-some, marvellous and beyond belief.

It thinks of you constantly, joy whom it loves. To you it ascends in desire. It falls in love with you, goes to you to beg for favours, overcomes by kissing, and melts in the fire of love.

Christ's lovers pay heed to no rank and desire no status in this life, so that they can be fervent and joyous in Christ's love and think more and more lovingly of him. God is truly infinite in greatness and better than ever we may think. His sweetnesses are uncounted; no created thing may ever really conceive him as he is; none of us can ever really comprehend him as he is in himself everlastingly. But when the mind begins to burn in desire for its Maker, it is able to receive uncreated light; it is so inspired and filled with gifts of the Holy Spirit, that—as far as this is possible for human beings—it is raised up to enjoy the sweetness of everlasting life. And, while the soul is filled with the sweetness of the Godhead and the heat of its Maker's light, and is offered and accepted in sacrifice to the everlasting King, it is as if quite consumed by fire.

Happy love, you are strong, ravishing, burning and unsatisfied. I want my soul whole and entire to be in your service and to think of nothing but you. Christ is the source of your love and we love him for himself alone. Whatever is to be loved is for Christ to whom we bring everything that we love.

Perfect love is truly present when the mind's whole intention and the innermost workings of the heart are lifted up into the love of God.

Love undivided and unique, your love is so great that you would never wish any sinner to be lost. It is not your will that the wicked should suffer. An untold sorrow should be more tolerable than a deadly sin. Therefore love God for himself and for no other reason. For how could God be all in each thing if there were any physical love of human beings in one of us?

Clear charity, enter me, take me into yourself, and present me thus before my Maker. You are a savour well tasted, a sweetness well smelled, a pleasant odour, a cleansing fire and an everlasting comfort. You enable us to contemplate; you open the gate of heaven for us. You close the mouths of our accusers, reveal goodness and hide a multitude of sins. We love you and preach you while we overcome the world by your means. We rejoice in you and ascend by means of your heavenly ladder.

Turn to me in your sweetness. I commend myself and those close to me to you for ever.

CONTEMPLATION

The contemplative life is divided into three parts: reading, prayer and meditation.

God speaks to us in reading. We speak to God in prayer. When we meditate, angels come down to teach us so that we do not go wrong. They ascend in prayer and offer our own prayers to God, rejoicing when all goes well for us, acting as messengers between us and God. Prayer is a humble desire of the mind turned toward God, which pleases him when it reaches him. Meditation on God and on godly things comes after reading, like the use of incense.

Reading depends on reason and inquiry into truth; it is like a good clear light shed on us. Prayer depends on praise and song, and contemplation is classed with prayer. Meditation relies on God's inspiration and understanding, his wisdom and aspiration.

If you ask what contemplation is, I find it very hard to define. There are those who say that the contemplative life is nothing but the knowledge of the future and of mysterious things, or study of God's words, or freedom from all external concerns. Others say that contemplation is freedom to see through the spectacles of wisdom, to a very high magnification indeed. Others say that it is a kind of treatise on wise looking at the soul, spread out as it were to see greatness. Others say rightly that contemplation is joy in heavenly things. Others say, with even greater justification, that it is the death of physical desires achieved by raising up the joys of the mind.

I think that contemplation means having in one's mind the joyful song of God's love and all the sweet praise of angels. We call this "jubilation," which is the goal of the prayer of perfection and of devotion in this life. That is the possession of the truly happy mind, which sees with spiritual eyes the Everlasting Lover and calls out with a loud voice in praise of him. It is the ultimate and really perfect form of death to this life. The psalm on the subject says: "Blessed the man who rejoices in contemplating God." None who are apart from God can rejoice in Jesus or taste the sweetness of his love unless they always desire to burn with the fire of everlasting love. Patiently and humbly, they must be made beautiful by cleansing of mind and body, to be adorned with spiritual jewels and raised up into contemplation, and unceasingly seek for healing virtues—which cleanse us from our wretched sins in this life and free us from all pain in the blessed endless life hereafter.

Even while exiled in this world you will be made worthy to feel the wonderful joy of God's love.

So don't be slow to check yourself by prayer and examination of conscience. Don't neglect spiritual meditation, for such spiritual works, and weeping and sorrow within, will surely kindle the fire of Christ's love in you, and all the virtues and gifts of the Holy Spirit will be poured into your heart. Begin with the practice of voluntary poverty, so that all you want in this world is to live soberly, chastely and humbly before God and humankind. Sometimes poverty causes us to have nothing, but it is a great virtue to wish to have nothing.

Of course we have many desires. Even the most perfect accept necessities, for no one would be perfect who refused to take the very basics that are necessary to staying alive.

The perfect man or woman must live thus: forsaking and despising everything for God's sake, and yet eating and wearing all that is necessary. If he or she has any want at any time, then there must be no complaint; love of God is the answer, and to refuse superfluity as far as possible.

The warmer you grow in the heat of everlasting light, the humbler in all hardship. Those who are truly meek despise themselves and are not provoked to anger. If we give ourselves up to meditation we can rise up to behold heavenly things by the acuity of our purified mind's eye; then, even if we fall ill, we shall be filled with heavenly joy. Then we do not stride out proudly, looking for external things, but rejoice only (but marvellously) in the sweetness of God's love, so wonderfully full of joy that we might well have been ravished in a dream!

That is the nature of contemplation, and, if we practise spiritual works long and assiduously, we shall reach the point where we contemplate everlasting things. The mind is so held that it sees shadows of heavenly things as in a glass, for while we live bv faith we see only as shadows, as if in a mirror. If our spiritual eye is open to that spiritual light, it may not see the light as it actually is, yet feel nevertheless that it is, and cleave to it with undreamed-of joy and heat. Hence the psalm says: "As its darkness, so its light."

Even though all the darkness of sin is departed from a holy soul, and the mind is purified and enlightened, while it is mortal it may not perceive perfect joy. Of course holy and contemplative people look on God with a clear vision (for their minds are opened and all barriers between God and them are thrown down); their hearts are purified and they see the inhabitants of heaven. Christ also gives us his consoling darkness and speaks to us in a pillar of cloud, but what we feel is truly joyful.

It is truly perfect love when anyone still mortal rejoices only in God, and wants nothing and desires nothing except God and for God's sake. And so we know that holiness does not consist in the crying out of the heart, or in tears, or in external works, but in the sweetness of perfect love and heavenly contemplation. Many people melt with tears yet suddenly turn to evil, but none will concern themselves with worldly things after truly tasting Everlasting Love.

Weeping and sorrow are proper to the unconverted and to beginners. Rejoicing in contemplation, however, is proper to the perfect alone. If we do penance for a long time, even though our conscience pricks us we surely feel that we have not as yet attained to perfect penance. Then our "tears are bread to us day and night," for as long as we punish ourselves with sighs and tears we have not reached the sweetness of contemplation.

We have to work very hard indeed to get contemplative sweetness, but when we do get it the joy is unbelievable. Of course it is not something that we can win by our own merit, but God's gift, and never yet, from the beginning of the world to this very day, has anyone ever been ravished in the contemplation of Everlasting Love without completely giving up all the vanities of this world.

What is more, we have to be experienced in sound, devout prayer, before contemplating heavenly joys.

Contemplation is a very pleasurable and desirable practice. It makes us glad and does us no harm. It makes us joyful, and we feel tiredness only when it departs from us.

Anyone who is inflamed by the fire of the Holy Spirit needs great rest of mind and body. Yet many people are unable to rest in mind because of all their pointless thoughts. They can't do as the psalmist says: "Rid yourself of worldly vanities and see that I am God."

These wandering hearts cannot taste and see how sweet our Lord is, they cannot savour the sweetness of the heights of contemplation. Every contemplative loves solitude, which is needed if the contemplative is not to be parted from his or her fervent desires.

Very contemplative persons are often thought to be fools, for their minds are so intent on unseen things, and so inflamed by the love of Christ, that the very stance of the body changes. Contemplatives seem to stand apart from all other human beings as children of God, and to other people seem raving mad.

While the soul gathers everything within itself in unending joy of love, it does not flow outward to physical things. Because it feeds on inward affections, it is hardly astonishing that it should sigh and say: "Who will give me you, my Brother, so that I can find you and kiss you?"

Devout souls who practise contemplation and are filled with everlasting love despise the vanities of this world, and want only to enjoy Jesus and to be in the splendid company of the angels, undisturbed by worldly changes and troubles.

There is nothing better and more joyful than the grace of contemplation, which lifts us out of the habits and practices of this world, and brings us to God. The grace of contemplation is nothing other than the being of joy. And what is perfect joy but grace confirmed in us, so that we stay joyful and happy in glorious eternity, living with saints and angels in endless joy? Above all it means knowing God truly, and loving him perfectly. It means seeing his Majesty shining, and in all eternity loving with wonderful joy and melody the God to whom be worship and joy with thanksgiving in the world of worlds. Amen.

Walter Hilton

St Peter's Church,
Thurgarton, the remnant of the ancient priory

WALTER HILTON

Walter Hilton, perhaps the most theologically adept of the medieval English mystics, has been admired for centuries as a wise and gentle spiritual guide. Details of his life, however, are quite scarce. He was born about 1330, possibly in north-central England, since the Hilton surname is fairly common in the counties of Nottinghamshire and Yorkshire. He apparently studied Canon Law at the University of Cambridge during that institution's first century and perhaps became a doctor of theology. Following his ordination as a priest, he lived the life of a hermit for a period, but seems to have found such a solitary life unsuitable and thereafter joined the monks of the Augustinian Order at the priory of St Peter in Thurgarton.

A distinctive feature of the Augustinian canons was the conviction that the sphere of their responsibilities lay not only within the monastic community, but extended into the secular world as well. The canons at Thurgarton Priory had a variety of such duties, including pastoral care in the nearby villages of Fiskerton and Lowdham, preaching ministries in the more distant cities of Nottingham and Leicester, and the administration of the priory's estates in Nottinghamshire, Derbyshire, and Lincolnshire. Hilton died at Thurgarton in 1395 or 1396 on the 24th of March, the Eve of the Annunciation, a day in the diocesan calendar on which this church is still remembered in prayer. There is some evidence that a shrine to Hilton was built at the priory, and that it served as a minor centre of pilgrimage.

The practical orientation of the Augustinians is also evident in Hilton's writings. His major work, *The Scale of Perfection*, probably the most widely read medieval devotional manual, is a book of practical guidance for fellow travellers on the spiritual path, advice offered with warmth, humility, and a depth of understanding that can come only from extensive personal experience. Hilton distinguishes two aspects or dimensions of inner re-formation on the gradual earthly journey of the Christian toward atonement, or union, with God. The first dimension, which he calls "reformation in faith," is simply the attempt to adhere to the basic beliefs and ethical standards of Christianity.

The second dimension, "reformation in feeling," is the realization of oneness with God, the dimension in which abstract beliefs become concrete realities. The first of these dimensions may be achieved easily and in a short time, the second only after a long time and with "great spiritual effort" (Book II, chs. 5 and 17).[1] But it is effort of a rather uncommon kind, designed as it is to transcend itself, to carry the seeker along the scale of spiritual perfection to the point where human effort is supplanted by divine activity and intention, a process of purification that is often a bit painful and disconcerting.[2] It consists of letting go of all things, of giving up striving for virtue, of becoming truly humble—of realizing "that you possess nothing, but are like an empty vessel that has no power to fill itself" (Book II, ch. 21). Disposing oneself to the Spirit is primarily a process of subtraction rather than addition.

The Scale is addressed to a nun living a solitary life, a "sister in the spirit in Jesus Christ," and contains some statements that a life of contemplative, or meditative, prayer is appropriate only for persons in such circumstances. But if we consider Hilton's writings as a whole, it is clear that he did not think that the practice of meditative prayer, leading to deep spirituality, should be limited to those who had separated themselves from society. As the title of another of his works—*Mixed Life*—suggests, he believed that persons active in the life of society (as were the Augustinians themselves to a degree) could, with diligent practice, open themselves to the life and transforming presence of the Spirit. When *The Scale* moved from manuscript to printed form in 1494, it began to reach a much wider audience and increased greatly in popularity among laypeople. Hilton's writings thus retain a relevance for modern travellers along these paths, whatever their circumstances or station in life.

The period during which Hilton lived was one of great social, political, and religious upheaval in Britain. But the foundations of the Thurgarton church and priory were laid in a more tranquil time long before this fourteenth-century turmoil. The priory was apparently founded around 1136 by Ralph Deincourt, a relative by marriage of William the Conqueror. Work on the priory, which was dedicated to "God and St Peter," was begun about 1140 and continued well into the thirteenth century.

The original priory consisted of a full range of monastic buildings, as well as a large church. These buildings provided ample accommodation for the communal religious life of sixty monks for almost four centuries, until the dissolution of the monasteries by King Henry VIII in the years following 1536. During these centuries the strength and influence of monasteries throughout Europe had gradually been declining and though they remained an important social, economic, and educational presence in many places, they were no longer the dominant cultural force they had been in the earlier Middle Ages. The Protestant Reformation brought severe criticism of monasticism as being unnecessary, ill-conceived, and, in many cases, corrupt, and led to the suppression of a great many monasteries on the Continent.

In England the Dissolution was motivated more by political power than by religious principles. The English monasteries had become quite wealthy and Henry VIII saw the opportunity, by dissolving them, an action supported by exaggerated claims of decadence and corruption, not only to replenish the royal treasury, but also to undermine further the authority of the pope. Two hundred of the smaller monasteries were declared dissolved in 1536. The dissolution of the larger ones, on a supposedly "voluntary" basis, was complete by 1540.

Most of the ex-monks received regular pensions and many eventually became secular clergymen. The pensions, and the prospects, for ex-nuns, were more limited, many going to live with their superiors or finding other informal, semi-monastic arrangements. The financial gain to the Crown was well over £100,000 a year, roughly doubling its annual income.

In 1536 Thurgarton Priory had at least sixteen canons, besides the prior, with an annual income of around £259, thus making it one of the larger religious houses. The document effecting its dissolution was signed on 12 June 1538 by the prior and eight of the canons, each of whom received a pension.[3]

Although the Protestant suspicion of monasticism continued throughout the seventeenth and eighteenth centuries, a sentiment strengthened by the Enlightenment, there has been an extraordinary revival of interest in the monastic life during the nineteenth and twentieth centuries. New communities have been founded around the world, including many in England and the United States, and new forms of monasticism have emerged, partly from the encounter of East and West, as many people attempt to return to the sources of Christian spirituality and to recover the mystical heart of their faith that warmed the souls, and bodies, of writers such as Walter Hilton.

The present church at Thurgarton, which was restored by Richard Milward in the middle of the nineteenth century, is the remaining remnant of the ancient Priory, the size and grandeur of which are reflected in the floor plan hanging near the north door. A list of the priors can be found on the pillar opposite this door.

Three pairs of original pillars, which apparently required decades to complete, have withstood the test of time and royal temerity. These support the nave, the tower, and the west wall. There were originally two towers, but with the Dissolution in the sixteenth century, one of them fell into ruin. The altar was dismantled following the Dissolution and the surface stone, which was probably quarried at Ancaster in the twelfth or thirteenth century, was rediscovered nearby in a well and was restored to its present and proper place during Milward's restoration work. The pulpit, lectern, and organ were also installed during this nineteenth-century restoration.

Just south of the priory lies Castle Hill, which is thought to be the location of a Saxon burial site and small fort. A stone coffin, along with several skeletons, was unearthed here by archeologists and presently sits outside the church. Castle Hill also has traces of a small chapel dating from the ninth or tenth century, thus extending the religious history of the area back some three centuries before the construction of the priory.

The village of Thurgarton is located in the county of Nottinghamshire, in the north-east Midlands, on the A612 main road midway between Nottingham and Newark-on-Trent. These can be approached via the M1 motorway or the A1 trunk road respectively. Both also have rail connections with London and Birmingham.

Notes

1. Citations, and the selections from *The Scale of Perfection* that follow, are a new translation, made using the 1927 version (London: Burns, Oates & Washbourne) and that by Gerard Sitwell (London: Burns & Oates, 1953). The "Letter to a Friend on hearing the Song of Angels" is from *The Cell of Self-knowledge* (Dublin: Gill and Macmillan; New York: Crossroad, 1981).

2. See Geraldine E. Hodgson, *English Mystics* (London: A. R. Mowbray, 1922. Reprint. Philadelphia: R. West, 1978), ch. 3, esp. pp. 116-17.

3. See David Knowles and R. Neville Hadcock, *Medieval Religious Houses: England and Wales* (New York: St. Martin's Press, 1971), pp. 144, 176.

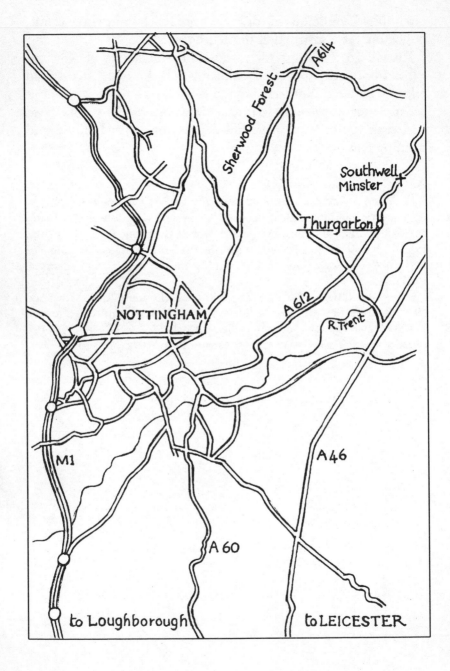

THE SCALE OF PERFECTION

Book I, Chapter 1

That the inner state of our soul should be like the outer

My sister in the spirit in Jesus Christ, I beg you to remain content and steadfast in the state to which the Lord has called you to serve him. Work hard with all the powers of your soul to be true to the good way of life you have embraced outwardly and inwardly. As you have turned away from the world, like a dead person physically turned to our Lord in the sight of others, let your heart be as it were dead to all earthly loves and fears, turned wholly to our Lord Jesus Christ. For you must know that turning one's body to God without the heart following is a mere semblance of virtue, devoid of truth.

Wretched indeed are those who neglect care of their inner selves, adapting only their outer selves to a form and appearance of holiness, in manners and dress, in the way they speak and how they go about their work; they judge what others do and find fault with them, thinking themselves to be really something when they are in fact nothing, and so deceiving themselves. Do not be like these, but turn both your heart and your body above all to God, and mould your inner self to God's likeness through humility, charity, and other virtues of the spirit; then you will be truly turned to God.

I am not saying that you will find it as easy, on the first day you enter [the religious life], to turn your soul through virtue as to shut your body up in a convent. You must know, though, that the purpose of enclosing your body like this is to enable you more easily to achieve an enclosure of the spirit. As your body is cut off from human converse, so can your heart be cut off from physical loves and all worldly fears. I shall now go on to describe, as it seems to me, how you can best achieve this.

CHAPTER 12

What binds Jesus to your soul and what separates him from it

Jesus is bound and held to your soul by good will and great desire for him alone, to hold him and see him in his spiritual bliss. The greater this desire, the closer Jesus is bound to your soul; the less it is, the looser the binding. Any feeling or inclination that lessens this desire and seeks to draw it away from steady concentration on Jesus and loving holding on to him, is not from God but is the work of the enemy, since it will separate Jesus from your soul. But if an inclination or feeling or revelation makes this desire greater, ties the knots of love and devotion to Jesus tighter, opens the eye of your soul to greater spiritual awareness, and increases humility, this is from God.

This should show you that you must not deliberately allow your heart to relax into, or take great pleasure in, physical sensations of this sort of comfort or delight, even if they are good in themselves; you must regard them as nothing or very little in comparison to spiritual longing for and steadfast meditation on Jesus, and not allow yourself to dwell on them overmuch.

CHAPTER 13

How contemplatives should occupy themselves

You must seek, rather, by working at prayer, to attain a spiritual sense of God, to gain wisdom from God, to know God's endless power, God's great goodness in himself and in his creatures: this is contemplation and the other is not. St Paul speaks of us being "rooted and grounded in love," so as to comprehend, not through hearing or tasting or any other physical sense, but through understanding, "with all the saints, what is the breadth and length and height and depth, and to know the love of Christ that surpasses knowledge, so that you may be filled with all the fullness of God" (Eph. 3:17-19).

Contemplatives must occupy themselves in knowing and spiritually comprehending these things, for they embrace the full knowledge of all spiritual things. This occupation is the one goal St Paul pressed on to achieve, as he says, "forgetting what lies behind and straining forward to what lies ahead, I press on toward the goal for the prize of the heavenly call of God in Christ Jesus" (Phil. 3:13-14). What lie behind are things of the body; what lie ahead are things of the spirit; so St Paul would forget all physical things, including his own body, in order to grasp the things of the spirit.

CHAPTER 14

How virtue begins in the understanding and the will and is perfected in love and affection

Now I have told you a little about contemplation and what it should be, so that you may recognize it, set it up as a target for your soul to aim at, and long for the rest of your life to achieve any part of it through the grace of our Lord Jesus Christ. This is how souls are conformed to God, which they cannot be unless they are first reformed through an abundance of virtue turned to affection— which means loving virtues because they are good in themselves.

Many have the virtues of humility, patience, charity to their fellow Christians and the like only in their understanding and will, with no spiritual delight in or love for them. These people often feel grouchy, reluctant and bitter at performing them, yet do so all the same, because their mind tells them to fear God. They have virtue in their understanding and will, but no love of them in their affections. But when—through the grace of Jesus and spiritual and physical exercises—understanding is turned into light and will into love, they then have virtues in their affections: they have chewed so hard on the bitter bark of the nut that they have broken through to the kernel, on which they can feed. This means that the virtues that were previously a burden to perform are now a true delight and pleasure; patience, purity, sobriety and charity are as enjoyable as anything.

*You cannot suddenly reform in faith and feeling, but only through grace
and long physical and spiritual effort*

The reformation I have spoken of is in faith, and can come
quickly. But after it comes reformation in faith and in feeling, and
this cannot be achieved lightly, but only through long effort and
great application. Reformation in faith is common to all the elect,
even if they are on the lowest rungs of charity. But reformation in
feeling is special to those souls capable of coming to a state of
perfection, and this does not come suddenly. Souls may come to
it only after receiving an abundance of grace and after great
spiritual effort; this is when they will first be helped out of their
spiritual sickness, and when all bitter passions and lusts of the
flesh and other old feelings are burned out of the heart by the fire
of desire, and other new grace-filled feelings are ushered in with
burning love and spiritual illumination. Then souls come very
close to perfection and to reformation in feeling. . . .

Souls cannot suddenly move from the lowest state to the highest, any more than a man starting to climb a ladder can put one
foot on the lowest rung and the next right up on the highest. He
has to put one foot after another on the next rung until he reaches
the top. The same is true of the spirit: we are not suddenly filled
with grace, but gradually, through long effort and careful practice, during which God, the source of all grace, helps and teaches
poor souls. No soul can be filled with grace without God's special
help and inner teaching.

CHAPTER 21

*How souls seeking this reformation will apply themselves and operate,
illustrated by a pilgrim going to Jerusalem*

Since you are looking for some way of operating that will bring
you closer to this reformation, let me tell you what seems to me
the shortest and handiest help I know of in this respect. I shall
illustrate how this is to be had by this story of a good pilgrim.

A certain man wants to go to Jerusalem, and because he does not know the way, he approaches another man who he hopes knows it better, and asks him how to get there. This other man tells him that he cannot get there without great discomfort and hard work, since the road is long and dangerous and filled with powerful thieves and robbers and all sorts of other dangers that can befall someone on the way. And also there are many roads that seem to lead there, but on them people are killed or robbed every day and cannot reach their destination. Nevertheless, there is one way that he can guarantee will lead all those who take it and keep to it to the city of Jerusalem, without being killed or dying on the way. They may often be robbed or sorely beaten and suffer much discomfort on the way, but their lives will be safe.

Then the pilgrim says: "If my life will be safe and I shall reach the destination I seek, I do not care what misfortune I may suffer on the way. So tell me what you can, and I promise to do as you say." The other answers him in these words: "Look, I am putting you on the right path. This is the way, and you must keep what I am telling you in mind. Whatever sounds, sights or feelings you chance upon on your way, do not willingly entertain them, sink into them, examine them, grow fond of them, or fear them, but keep to your path, thinking only that you want to get to Jerusalem. That is your aim, your desire, and nothing else but that. And if you are robbed, beaten, scorned, despised, do not fight back if you want to keep your life and suffer no more harm, but accept the harm done to you and go on as though nothing had happened. And if people try to delay you with stories and tempt you with other prospects, so as to make you laugh and abandon your pilgrimage, turn a deaf ear and do not answer; say only that you want to be in Jerusalem. And if they offer you gifts and try to make you rich in worldly goods, take no notice of them; think constantly of Jerusalem. And if you keep to this way and do what I have said, I guarantee that your life will be safe and you will reach the destination you desire."

The spiritual meaning of the story is this: Jerusalem signifies a sighting of peace and means contemplation in perfect love of God. For contemplation is nothing other than sighting God, who is perfect peace. So if you want to reach this sighting of real peace and be a true pilgrim to Jerusalem, I shall—though I cannot put myself in your place—set you as far as I can on the way there. The start of the high road you have to follow is reformation in faith, humbly grounded in the faith and laws of Holy Church, as I have said before: you can be sure that, even if you have previously sinned, provided that you are now reformed by the sacrament of penance according to the rites of the Church, you are on the right path.

Now, once you are on the safe path, if you want to speed up your journey and make good progress, you must keep two things in mind: humility and love. This means telling yourself that you are nothing, have nothing, seek nothing, except one thing. You must keep the meaning of these words always in your intentions and in the purpose of your soul, even if you do not specially call them to mind, which is not necessary. Humility says: "I am nothing, I possess nothing." Love says: "I seek nothing except one thing, and that is Jesus." These two strings, well fastened with the mind of Jesus, play a good harmony on the harp of the soul, when skilfully plucked with the finger of understanding; the lower you pluck the first, the higher the second sounds. The less you feel yourself to be or to possess on your own, through humility, the more you long to possess of Jesus, in the desire of love. . . .

Just as true pilgrims going to Jerusalem leave behind house and land, wife and children, making themselves poor and bereft of all possessions in order to travel lightly the whole way, so, if you would be a spiritual pilgrim, you must divest yourself of all that you possess, good deeds and bad, and cast them all behind you; you must become so poor in your own estimation that there is nothing of your own doing that you can rely on: just desire ever more grace and love, and seek always the spiritual presence of Jesus. If you do this, then you will set your heart fully on getting to Jerusalem and nowhere else but there. This means that you will set your heart entirely on having nothing but the love of Jesus, and the spiritual sighting of him that he will give you; that alone is what you have been created and redeemed for, and that is your beginning and your end, your joy and your bliss. . . .

Now you are on your way and know the name of the place you are heading for. Set out, then, on your journey. Starting out is nothing but spiritual exercise, and physical also, when needed: carry them out in a manner suited to you, as I shall show you. I consider that the best thing for you to undertake is what is suited to your physical and spiritual level or state, provided it helps your grace-given desire to love Jesus and makes this easier, more complete, and leading more directly to all the virtues and all goodness; it might be preaching, or meditating, or reading, or physical labour. As long as what you do is what most strongly binds your heart and will to the love of Jesus, and draws your inclinations and thoughts farthest from worldly vanity, it is good for you to do it. But if you find that custom is making what you are doing stale, and that something else would profit you more and put you more in the way of grace, then put aside what you are doing and take up something else. Although your desire and heart's longing for Jesus should never change, the spiritual exercises you use in praying or meditating to nourish your desire may vary, and may well change once you feel yourself urged by grace to apply your own heart. Your doings and desire work like sticks and fire: the more sticks you lay on the fire, the greater the blaze; so the more different spiritual exercises you can devise in your mind to keep your desire whole, the more burning will be your longing for God. So consider carefully what you can do best, what will be most helpful in keeping your desire for Jesus whole, provided it is something you are free to do without breaking the common law, and do that.
. . . .

CHAPTER 44

The secret voice of the Lord in the soul

Our Lord Jesus says this of those who love him: "My sheep hear my voice.... I know my own and my own know me" (John 10:27, 14). The secret voice of Jesus is fully true, and it makes souls true. There is no pretence of fantasy in it, no pride or hypocrisy, but only gentleness, humility, peace, love, solidarity; it is full of life, love and grace. So, when Jesus' voice sounds in souls, the effect is sometimes so powerful that they immediately put aside everything in them by way of praying, speaking, reading or meditating (as mentioned earlier), and all sorts of physical activity, and listen fully to the voice, hearing and taking in the sweet sound of this spiritual voice with relaxation and love, snatched away, as it were, from all earthly things.

When this happens, Jesus shows himself sometimes as a master to be feared, sometimes as a father to be revered, and sometimes as a spouse to be loved. His voice keeps souls in wonder-filled reverence and in the lovely sight of him, which souls love at the time and never so much as then. They feel such security and comfort in Jesus, and enjoy so much of his goodness, that they would have it always so and never do anything else. They think they are touching Jesus and that through the power of this indescribable touch they are made whole and stable in themselves, reverently seeing nothing but Jesus, as though nothing existed besides Jesus and themselves, held up only by the enjoyment and wonderful goodness of Jesus, by what they see and feel. . . .

CHAPTER 46

Hearing the hidden word of God

All this loving dalliance of secret speech between Jesus and souls may be called a hidden word, as scripture describes it: "Now a word came stealing to me, my ear received the whisper of it" (Job 4:12). Jesus' inspiration is a hidden word, since it is secretly hidden from all who love the world and revealed only to those who love him; through it, pure souls easily hear the whisper, which is a special revelation of God's truthfulness. Each and every grace-given understanding of truthfulness felt with inward enjoyment and spiritual delight is Jesus whispering secretly in the ear of pure souls. They need to be very pure and humble and to possess all the other virtues, and to be half deaf to the jangling noises of the world, if they are properly to hear these sweet spiritual whispers. . . . Such revelations, truthfully grounded in grace and

humility, make souls wise and burning with desire to see Jesus
face-to-face.

These are the spiritual matters I spoke of earlier, which can be
called new feelings brought by grace. I have spoken of them but
briefly, to show your soul something of them. Souls that are
wholly inspired by grace to experience these things can learn more
in an hour of such spiritual matters than can be written in a book,
however long.

LETTER TO A FRIEND
on hearing
THE SONG OF ANGELS

My dear friend in Christ,

From what you have told me and what I have heard from a mutual friend, I understand that you would like to have more knowledge and understanding of what is meant by "the song of angels," or divine harmony. I believe you want to know what it is, how it can be felt in a person's soul, and how one can be sure that it is real and not imagination. Also how one can tell whether it comes from a good spirit and is not put into a person's soul by the wiles of an evil spirit.

It would be nice to be able to tell you everything you want to know about these things, but quite honestly I can't be sure what the real truth of the matter is. Let me try, though, to tell you briefly what I think.

You must know that the aim and fulfilment of perfection consist of union between God and a person's soul through perfect charity. This union is brought about when the powers of the soul are brought by grace to that state of elevation that we call the "highest stage." This is when the mind is firmly fixed, without deviating or wandering, on God and the things of the spirit, when the reason has been purged of all concerns of the world and the flesh, when the mind no longer dwells on human ideas and imaginings, but is so enlightened by grace that it can contemplate God and spiritual things; when the will and the affections have been cleansed and stripped of all human and carnal love, and are inflamed with a burning love of the Holy Spirit.

No one, you understand, can remain in this state of union all the time or to the full extent in this life, because a mortal body cannot support it: for that we have to wait for the bliss of heaven. But the degree to which a soul can approach this unity in this life indicates the stage of perfection it has reached. The more it comes, through grace, to resemble the image and likeness of its Creator in this way, the greater joy and happiness it will possess in heaven.

The Lord our God is eternal and unchanging, his mighty power cannot fail, he is the height of wisdom and light, pure truth without error or distortion, absolute goodness and love, total peace and delight. So the more a soul is joined and united to our Lord, made like and turned into him, the more stable and powerful it becomes, the wiser and more enlightened it is, the greater goodness and peace it enjoys, the more loving and virtuous it will be—the more perfect, in a word. A soul that through the grace of Jesus, and through long practice of physical and spiritual exercises, has overcome and rooted out desires, passions and unreasonable impulses—the inner ones of the mind and the outer ones of the senses—and has cultivated all the virtues—humility and meekness, patience and gentleness, firmness and steadfastness, self-control, wisdom, truth, hope and love—will have become as perfect as it can in this life.

Such a soul will then receive all manner of favours from our Lord: not only in its secret innermost nature, thanks to the union it enjoys with our Lord, which consists in knowing and loving God, burning with clear and spiritual love of him, being changed into the Godhead; it will also enjoy many other spiritual comforts and delights, and savour the sweetness of divine favour in all sorts of ways by which our Lord reveals his presence to his creatures here on earth, and through which the soul can grow and gain in charity. Sometimes, God gives such love to a soul that it is purified to the point where the whole of creation, all that can be seen or heard or felt by any of the senses, becomes a source of pleasure and joy; the senses find a new delight and inspiration in all created things. Whereas before the impulses of the senses had been tainted with original sin, so that they were hollow and evil, they are now spiritual and pure, so that they need give rise to no remorse or reproach from one's conscience.

This shows the goodness of God: where earlier a person had been punished in his or her sensuality, so that the body was made to share in the sufferings of the soul, now the soul is able to delight in the senses, and the body can share in the joy and pleasure of the soul—in a spiritual, not physical way—just as it had shared in its sufferings. This is when human beings recover, through grace, their freedom and dignity, above that of the rest of creation, when they can see the rest of creation as it really is; when, that is, they come to see and hear and feel God alone in the whole of creation. This is when the senses become spiritual through all-embracing love, when they become part of the inner being of the soul.

Then, too, our Lord gives the soul the privilege of hearing the divine harmony. There is no physical simile by which this can be described, because it belongs to the realm of the spirit and is beyond the powers of our imagination or reason. A soul can feel it and experience it, but cannot demonstrate it. I shall try, nevertheless, to tell you something about it to the best of my ability.

When a soul has been purified by God's love, enlightened in its understanding, established by his power, then its vision is opened to the things of the spirit and it can see virtues in angels and the holy souls and other heavenly things. Its purity enables it to feel the touch and hear the voice of good spirits—I mean it can do this spiritually, not physically. And once a soul has been lifted, seized up, out of its senses, and beyond consciousness of physical things, then, in transports of love and enlightenment (God willing) it can hear and feel the divine harmony, which is the sound of the heavenly choirs of angels adoring God.

Hearing this divine harmony is not the greatest privilege a soul can enjoy. Because the impurity of a human soul, bound to a body, makes it unlike the angels, it cannot hear this harmony except through the cleansing power of love; it needs to be completely purified and totally filled with love before it can hear this heavenly sound. But the greatest and most particular joy the soul can experience is the love of God in himself and for himself; seeing and communing with angels and other spiritual beings is secondary. Just as a soul can sometimes be helped to understand spiritual matters by the spirit working through human imagination, as the prophet Ezekiel saw the truth of God's hidden mysteries in his human imagination, so the spirit can help a soul caught up in the love of God to escape from all material and bodily sensations to a heavenly joy, in which it can hear the divine harmony, the angels' song of praise, provided it has attained to a high enough degree of love.

It seems to me impossible for a soul to hear the angels' song, the divine harmony, without being perfect in love; on the other hand, it is possible to be perfect in love without hearing it. For this, the soul has to be so consumed in the crucible of love that all physical elements have been burned out of it, and anything that can come between this soul and the purity of the angels has been removed and taken away from it. Then indeed can this soul "sing a new song to the Lord"; then it can really hear the blessed harmony of heaven, the angels' chorus of praise, without pretending or being deceived.

Our Lord knows which souls have this burning love to such a degree that they can hear the divine harmony. What is essential for anyone who wants to hear it, without self-deceit or the tricks of the imagination or the wiles of the devil, is to have perfect love. This means that all false love and fear, all false joy and sorrow, have been expunged from the heart, so that it can love nothing but God, fear nothing but God, have no joy or sorrow in anything but God. Anyone who follows this road by God's grace can be sure of being on the right way.

But it is possible to be deceived by one's imagination, or by our enemy the devil, in this matter. Some people who have striven for a long time to get rid of their sins and acquire virtues through physical mortification and spiritual exercises may perhaps come to peace of mind and a clear conscience; they may then abandon their prayers, bible readings and meditations on the passion of Christ, and cease to be conscious of their own wretchedness. Then, before God summons them in his own time, they take hold of their mind by the scruff of the neck, as it were, and force it to see the things of heaven, or, before grace has made their senses truly spiritual, they can over-stress their minds through imagination to such an extent that they overtax their brains by excess effort and end up by destroying the powers and wits of body and soul. Then it will be feeble-mindedness that makes them think they hear marvellous sounds and songs. In fact, this will be pure fantasy, brought on by their deranged minds, as those who are in the grip of madness always think they can hear and see things no one else can. This is either nothing but empty-headed fantasy, or it is the work of the devil putting the hearing of such sounds into their imagination. If you introduce presumption into your imagination and actions, and so become prey to disordered fantasies, like mad people, without the ordering of the mind that grace brings, and without the support of spiritual strength, then the way is open for the devil to come into your soul and deceive you with his false enlightenment, false sounds and false comforts.

A soul then becomes the false ground in which error and heresy can flourish, along with false prophecy, presumption and false reasoning, blasphemy, slander and a load of other evils. So if you see anyone concerned with spiritual matters fall into this error and self-deception, or in a frenzy of false rapture, you can be sure that he or she is not hearing the divine harmony and never has done. Those who really hear it become so prudent that their imagination will not lead them astray, and they will be proof against the crafty workings of the devil.

Some people feel what seems like a heavenly sound or some sort of sweet sound, in their hearts; this can sometimes be good but can sometimes be deceptive. It happens like this: they set their hearts to think only of the name of Jesus, hold their thoughts constantly on this, and in due course the name becomes a source of comfort and peace, so that they think they can "hear" the name playing sweet music in their hearts. The pleasure they derive from this is so great that all the faculties of their souls are submerged in it. If they are really hearing this sound and feeling this peace in their hearts, then this is a good thing and comes from God, and you can be sure that as long as they remain humble, they will not be deceived. This is not the divine harmony, but the soul rejoicing through the offices of the good spirit.

When a soul truly and humbly offers itself to Jesus, putting all its trust and hope in him and keeping him constantly in mind, then the Lord will, if he so desires, purify the soul's feelings, filling it with the sweetness of his presence, which will taste to the soul's feelings like honey, sing in them like sound, and be anything sweet to the soul, so that its longing for evermore is to cry out the name of Jesus. Then it will also find comfort in the psalms and hymns and anthems of the Church's worship, and enjoy singing them freely and heartily, without discord or reluctance. This is a good thing, and a gift from God, since it derives from love of Jesus, which is strengthened and refreshed by such songs of praise.

But you must be wary of a false feeling of security in such feelings; not so much when your feelings are singing to Jesus and loving him for the sweetness of his presence in your soul, but afterwards, when the moment has passed, and your heart's ardour is cooling: this is the time to beware of self-importance. You can also be led astray through being told that it is good to keep the name of Jesus, or some other divine word, in your mind; you can then make enormous efforts to do so, and teach yourself to have it always on call in your mind, but without any feeling of sweetness in your heart, of any light of knowledge in your understanding; it will be a mere abstract thought of God, or Jesus, or Mary, or any other good word. Deceit can enter in here, not that it is wrong to bear Jesus constantly in mind, but there is the danger of taking what is only a habit of mind acquired by one's own efforts for a special divine favour, and so giving it more value than it has. You must know that any abstract concept of Jesus, or of any spiritual matter, without any feeling of love or light of understanding, is a blindness and deception if you take it for more than it is worth. It is safer to be humbler in your own mind and regard it as of no value, till your feelings are fired with love, and your understanding enlightened with knowledge.

There, I have told you something about this, I think. I am sure there is more to say, and I am not sure that all I have said is correct. If you think differently, or if others are inspired by grace to contradict me, let me leave you with this thought (and leave the word to others): for me, the main thing is to rely on faith and not on feelings.

The Cloud
of Unknowing

*Clouds over a typical church
of the north-east Midlands*

THE CLOUD OF UNKNOWING

Although *The Cloud of Unknowing* is one of the most well-known and best-loved English mystical works, the identity of its author remains unknown. Evidence of contemporary literary influences on the author, as well as of his influence on other spiritual writers such as Walter Hilton, indicate that *The Cloud* was written in the latter part of the fourteenth century, possibly around 1370. Stylistic evidence suggests strongly that the work was composed in the north-east Midlands, that is, somewhere in the vicinity of Leicestershire or Nottinghamshire. The author was probably a priest, perhaps a Carthusian monk, and was well versed in the religious literature of his day. More than this we cannot say with certainty.

The Cloud was addressed specifically to a young man of twenty-four who apparently had recently entered a religious Order. But it is clear from the Prologue that the author realized that the book, either through accident or intention, would be likely to find a wider audience. Thus he says here that while any pearls of spiritual wisdom that may be contained in the pages of his book should not be cast before the spiritually insensitive, there are those who are active in secular society who are sincerely interested and equipped for deep prayer and his book "should by God's grace be a great source of strength for them."[1]

David Knowles has said that the special significance of *The Cloud* lies in its being "the earliest instance in any vernacular literature of a direct, practical, non-schematic instruction in the entrance and progress in the contemplative life understood (as it has been ever since) as the life of mystical, infused prayer."[2] In developing his approach, the author draws explicitly on the mystical theology of the fifth-century writer known as Pseudo-Dionysius, who was perhaps a Syrian monk, but was considered in the Middle Ages to have been the convert of St Paul's mentioned in Acts 17:34. This master's teaching that there are two ways of knowing God—the rational and the mystical—is a central theme of *The Cloud*.

Rational knowledge of God consists in having beliefs or concepts about God; mystical knowledge consists of acquaintance with or experience of God's being or presence, which cannot be captured in any concept. Mystical knowledge, the way of love, fulfills and immeasurably surpasses rational knowledge, the way of thought, because "He can be taken and held by love but not by thought" (ch. 6). The work of contemplation, then, involves looking beyond mental activity, by placing all thoughts and words and images underneath a "cloud of forgetting," and directing one's wholehearted attention and intention toward the "cloud of unknowing" where God lies hidden. Such work is not easy; it consists in forgetting and letting go of the self, of transcending the ego, of moving beyond one's mind.

While the author emphasizes that mystical knowledge cannot be attained simply through sufficient human effort, and therefore is hesitant to recommend specific contemplative techniques, he does suggest a few for his reader to test the usefulness of. The most notable of these devices, the one that is likely to be the most familiar to modern readers, is concentration on the sound of a single word, such as "God," "love," or perhaps "maranatha."[3] This method of what would now be known as the mantra is a way of going beyond thoughts and words by focussing one's attention wholly on only one word. It is therefore a method of becoming poor in spirit, of giving up the distracting richness of memories, images, and thoughts that adorns and sustains our minds, and living for a while, inwardly naked and pure of heart, in the poverty of a single thought, a single sacred word. As John Cassian, the fifth-century monk who was instrumental in bringing the spiritual methods of Eastern Christianity into the Western tradition, has said, the poverty of the mantra is a "grand poverty" that is a key to the kingdom. And as the author of *The Cloud* suggests, if we can learn to focus all of our intensity in "the height and the depth, and the length and the breadth of our spirit" (ch. 39) on the chosen word, we will gradually come to experience the reality it signifies.

Christians of all persuasions and denominations emphasize, of course, that surrendering to the Spirit is what is most needed. But what many of these traditions lack, and what the Christian mystical tradition offers, is a specific method of doing so. If we can learn to speak a sacred word, to speak it wholeheartedly and let it loosen the shackles of the self, we will have found a way of becoming still and knowing what cannot be thought, of suffering a death and resurrection, of dying daily, hourly, from moment to moment.

The author encourages his reader to "beat with a sharp dart of longing love upon this cloud of unknowing which is between you and your God. Avoid thinking of anything under God and do not leave this exercise no matter what happens. For it alone, of itself, destroys the root and the ground of sin" (ch. 12). The nurturing of this longing love, a spark that will become a flame, is the essence of the contemplative path revealed here. It will burn away the root of sin, which manifests itself in what are today classified into a vast array of neurotic and psychosomatic disorders that imprison us within ourselves and diminish the depth and quality of our lives.

But this "humble impulse of love" not only fuels inner freedom through a kind of divine psychotherapy, it transforms morality from a duty into a spontaneous inclination, "for when it is truly implanted, all the virtues will be perfectly and delicately implanted, experienced and contained in it, without any mixture of motive" (ch. 12). Here the author reveals the social value and dimension of contemplation: "This blind impulse of love towards God for himself alone, this secret love beating on this cloud of unknowing, is . . . of more use to all your friends both bodily and spiritually" than engaging in any form of rational activity (ch. 9). Indeed, "we cannot know how wonderfully all people dwelling on earth are helped by this exercise" (ch. 3). The apparent inwardness of contemplative prayer, far from being silent self-absorption, is an inwardness leading outward. It is a way of finding ourselves through losing ourselves, of finding the freedom necessary for true human contact and for a fuller and fresher engagement with the whole of reality.

The north-east Midlands lie in the heart of England, the land of Sherwood Forest, where the River Trent winds through rural countryside dotted by countless golden-hued stone churches and villages. This area, consisting primarily of the counties of Leicestershire and Nottinghamshire, is served by two major highways— the M1 to the west and the A1 to the east, the latter in part following the old Roman Ermine Street. Thurgarton Priory is here, and while some scholars have suggested that Walter Hilton was perhaps *The Cloud*'s author, subsequent scholarship has effectively laid this theory to rest. *The Cloud* conveys little of the social, economic, or political turbulence of the fourteenth century, but seems, rather, to reflect the gentleness and serenity of the Midlands landscape.

Notes

1. Citations above are from *The Cloud of Unknowing*, edited, with an Introduction by James Walsh (New York: Paulist Press, 1981). The extracts that follow are in a new version made specially for this book.

2. David Knowles, *The English Mystical Tradition* (London: Burns & Oates; New York: Harper & Brothers, 1961), p. 99.

3. See John Main, *The Inner Christ* (London: Darton, Longman and Todd, 1987).

THE CLOUD OF UNKNOWING

My friend in the spirit in God, I beg and pray you to pay the utmost attention to how you carry out your vocation. Give thanks to God with all your heart, so that, with the help of God's grace, you may stand firm against all the cunning attacks of your bodily and spiritual enemies, and so win the everlasting crown. Amen.

* * * * *

CHAPTER 1

My spiritual friend in God, in my humble opinion there are four levels of Christian living, these being: Common, Special, Singular and Perfect. Three of these can be started and ended in this life, and the fourth can, through grace, be started here, but it ends in the everlasting bliss of heaven. Just as you see the order in which I have placed them here, first Common, then Special, then Singular and finally Perfect, so do I believe our Lord in his great mercy has called you to follow them in this order and has led you to him through your heart's desire.

With regard to the first, as you well know, when you were living on the first, common, level, with your worldly friends, I believe that God's everlasting love, through which he made you and fashioned you when you were nothing, and then redeemed you through his precious blood when you were lost in Adam, would not allow you to be so far from God in this state and on this level of life. And so God kindled your desire by his grace, and fastened it with a leash of loving longing, with which he led you into a more special state and way of life, to be a servant of his special servants; here you can learn to live more specially and more spiritually than you did, or could do, on your previous common level of living.

What then? It seems God would still not leave you there, out of the great love he has had for you since your conception. So what did God do? Can't you see how sweetly and gracefully he has secretly pulled you up to the third degree, the singular? In this solitary way of life you can learn to pick up your love's feet, to

71

march toward the state and level of life called perfect, the final state.

CHAPTER 3

Lift up your heart humbly to God in love, fixing your attention on God alone and not his creation. Learn to hate thinking about anything other than God, so that the whole purpose of your mind and will is fixed on God alone. Make yourself forget all God's creatures and their works, so that your thoughts and desires are not directed or drawn to any of them, in general or in particular. Leave them alone, casually; take no notice of them.

This is how the soul is most pleasing to God. This is the task the saints and angels delight in and strive to advance with all their might. All the demons go mad when you perform it, and seek every way of defeating you in it. All those living on earth are helped by your performing this task, to an amazing degree, though you do not know how. Even the souls in Purgatory are relieved of their suffering by what you do. And nothing else can so purify you and make you virtuous. If your soul is helped by grace in the desires of its senses, the task will be light and soon performed; without this help you will find it amazingly difficult.

CHAPTER 4

. . . All beings with the gift of reason, angels and ourselves, have in each of them one main faculty, that of knowing, and another, that of loving. By the first, that of knowing, God who made the angels and us remains ever unknowable; by the second, that of loving, however, God can be understood fully—though in a different way by each one of us—to the extent that a single loving soul can, by virtue of its love, comprehend the One who is fully sufficient—and incomparably more so—to fill all the souls and angels that can exist. This is the endless marvellous miracle of love, worked out without ceasing, since God performs it all the time and shall never cease to do so. Let those who can see this by grace do so: to experience this is endless bliss, not to do so is endless suffering.

This is why those who have been re-made by grace so as to pay continual heed to the promptings of God's will, rather than the promptings of their own nature, will never in this life lack some foretaste of endless bliss, nor the full substance of it in heaven. So do not be surprised that I encourage you in this task, because this is what we would have done had we never sinned. This is what we were made for, and all things were made for us, to help us pursue this. If we do this, we shall be made whole again; if we do not, we shall fall deeper and deeper into sin, and farther and farther from God. It is only by continual attending to and striving to perform this task, and this alone, that we can rise higher and higher from sin, and nearer and nearer to God.

So take good care how you spend your time, for nothing is more precious than time. In a moment, however short, heaven can be won or lost. To show you how precious time is, just think that God, who is the giver of time, never gives two times together, but one after another. God does this because he would never alter the order or fixed course of his creation. Time is made for us, not us for time. . . .

Do not think, because I speak of darkness or a cloud, that I am talking about any cloud formed from the vapours that fly about in the air, or any darkness such as that in your house at night, when your candle has gone out. You can picture such darkness or clouds with your imagination, calling them to mind on the brightest summer day, or picture a clear shining light on the darkest day of winter. Leave such imaginings aside; they are not what I am talking about. When I say "darkness," I mean an absence of knowing, with everything you do not know, or have forgotten, dark to you, unseen by the eye of your spirit. This is why I call it, not a cloud of the air, but a cloud of unknowing, between you and your God.

CHAPTER 5

If you ever reach this cloud, stay in it and work in it as I tell you to. You must, since this cloud of unknowing is above you, between you and your God, put a cloud of forgetting below you, between you and all beings ever made. You may perhaps think you are very far from God, since this cloud of unknowing is between you and your God, but if you think about it, you are still farther from God when you have no cloud of forgetting between you and all beings ever made. And when I say, "all beings ever made," I mean not only the beings themselves, but all their works and states. I make no exception for any creature, bodily or spiritual, or for any state they may be in or anything they may produce, good or evil. In short, all have to be hidden under the cloud of forgetting.

Even if it is useful sometimes to think what certain special beings are and do, it is of little or no use in carrying out this task. Calling any beings God ever made, or their deeds, to mind, is a sort of spiritual seeing, because the eye of your soul is opened and fixed on them, as the archer's eye is fixed on his target. I tell you this: everything you think of is above you at the time and so between you and your God. And whatever you have in your mind except God puts you that much farther from God.

Indeed—if I may be allowed to say so—in carrying out this task, it is of little or no use even to think of God's goodness or worth, or of Our Lady, or of the saints or angels in heaven, or of the joys of heaven. I mean: thinking with a special regard for them, as though doing so could further your purpose. I do not believe it can in any way do so. Although it is good to think of God's goodness, and to love and praise him for it, it is nevertheless far better to think of God's naked being, and to love and praise God for himself.

CHAPTER 6

Now you will ask me: "How shall I think of God in himself, and what is God?" I can give you no answer to this, except: "I don't know."

Your question has led me into the very darkness, the very cloud of unknowing, that I want you to be in. Through grace, we can fully know and think of all other beings and their works—yes, even of God's works—but no one can think of God. So I would let go of everything I can think of, and choose what I cannot think of as my love. Indeed, God may be loved, but not thought. Love can grasp and hold God; thought never can. And so, while it may sometimes be good to think about God's goodness and worth in particular, while it may be illuminating and form part of contemplation, in performing this task you must still cast this aside and cover it with the cloud of forgetting. And you have to walk above it determinedly, but also with desire, with a devout and pleasing urge of love, and try to pierce the darkness above you. Then smite the thick cloud of unknowing with a sharp spear of longing love, and stay in it whatever may happen.

CHAPTER 9

The sharp promptings of your intelligence, which will always press in on you when you engage in this blind task, must always be held in check; unless you hold them in check, they will hold you in check. In fact, when you are convinced that you are in this darkness, and that there is nothing in your mind but God, if you really look, you will find that your mind is not occupied with this darkness, but has a clear image of something lower than God. If this is the case, then that something is above you for the time being, and between you and God. So put such clear images from you, however holy and pleasing they may be. I tell you this: it is more beneficial to the health of your soul, more worthwhile in itself and more pleasing to God and to all the saints and angels in heaven—not to mention all your worldly and spiritual friends, living and dead—to have a blind urge of love for God in himself, an unseeing settling on this cloud of unknowing, to have this and feel it with your spiritual senses, than to have the eye of your soul open to contemplating or gazing on all the angels and saints in heaven, or to be hearing all the joyful melodies that accompany them in their bliss. . . .

This is not to say that any such sudden, naked thought of any good, pure spiritual thing below God, which pushes itself into your will or understanding, or which you deliberately draw on yourself in order to increase your devotion (even if it hinders the task in hand) is evil of itself. No, God forbid that you should think so! But I am saying that even if it is good and holy, it is more of a hindrance than a help in this task—while you are engaged on it, that is. There is no doubt that those who seek God perfectly cannot ultimately be content with thoughts of any angel or saint in heaven.

CHAPTER 12

So, if you want to stand and not fall, never give in, but beat unceasingly on this cloud of unknowing that stands between you and your God with a sharp spear of longing love. Hate the thought of anything below God, and do not be distracted by anything that may happen. This alone is the task that destroys the ground and root of sin. However much you fast, however early you rise, however scratchy your hairshirt; more, even if you were allowed to—which you are not—put out your eyes, cut the tongue out of your mouth, bung up your ears and nostrils, chop off your limbs and do every manner of injury to your body that you can think of, all this would be of no avail to you. The ferment of sin and the stirrings of the flesh will still be with you, like it or not, as long as you live.

What more can I say? However much you weep out of sorrow for your sins, or on account of Christ's passion, however much you think about the joys of heaven, what good will this do you? It will of course be good, helpful, beneficial, and gain you grace. By comparison with the blind urge of love, however, it will or can do little without this. This in itself is the better part Mary chose, without the rest. Those who do not have it can gain little or no benefit. Not only does it cut away the ground and root of sin, here and now; it also obtains virtues. Because if you think about it properly, all virtues will be carefully and perfectly conceived, felt and included in this, without confusing your intention in any way. And however many virtues we may possess without this, they are bound to be confused with some deviant intention, which makes them imperfect.

Virtue is nothing other than "an ordered and measured affection,"* plainly directed toward God for his own sake. God in himself is the sole cause of all virtues; so much so, that if anyone is moved to a virtue by any cause confused with God—even if God is the main cause—then that virtue is imperfect. This can be seen, for example, in the virtues of meekness and charity as compared to all the others: those who have them to the full do not need any more; they have them all.

CHAPTER 26

So, work steadily for a while, and beat against this high cloud of unknowing, and then rest. But those who undertake this task will truly find it hard work, really hard, unless they are given a very special grace, or else have been engaged on it for a long time.

But where, you may ask, does this hard work lie? Certainly not in that devout urge of love continually brought about in their will, not by themselves, but by the hand of Almighty God, who is always ready to carry out this task in the souls of all those who set themselves to it, who do all that is in their power, and have done so for a long time, to enable them to carry it out.

Where, then, is this work, tell me? It lies entirely in treading down the thought of all beings God ever made, in holding them down under the cloud of forgetting I spoke of earlier. The work is all in this, for this is what we have to do, with the help of grace. The higher thing—the urge of love, that is—is God's work alone. So if you go on doing your work, I promise you God will certainly not fail in his.

Work on determinedly, then: let me see how you stand up to the task. Can't you see how God stands fast and supports you? Shame on you! Just work hard for a while, and you will soon be relieved of the main burden of this task. Although it will be hard and difficult at first, when you have no devotion, later, when you have devotion, what was formerly so hard for you will become

---

*A definition made several times by Richard of St Victor, e.g. Benjamin Minor, ch. 7: *Nihil aliud est virtus quam animi affectus ordinatus et moderatus.*

easy and light. Then you will have little or no work to do, because God will sometimes do all the work himself, though not always, and not for long at a time, but as and when he pleases; when he does, you will take pleasure in letting him get on with it.

Then, if you are fortunate, God may sometimes send out a beam of spiritual light, piercing the cloud of unknowing that stands between you and him, and show you some of his secrets, which we may not and cannot tell. Then you will feel yourself set on fire by the flame of God's love, to an extent I cannot describe—or may or will not at this time. I dare not take upon myself to speak of the work that belongs to God alone with my blabbering fleshly tongue: even if I dared, I would not do so. But I enjoy telling you of our part in the task, when we feel ourselves urged and helped by grace: this is the less perilous of the two.

CHAPTER 29

Those who desire to regain the purity they have lost through sin, and to achieve a well-being free from all distress, must persevere in this task, and suffer the pains it brings, whoever they are, whether hardened sinners or not sinners at all.

It is hard work for everyone—sinners and innocents who have never sinned much alike. But it is far harder for those who have been sinners than for those who have not, as you would expect. Nevertheless, it sometimes happens that those who have been dreadful and habitual sinners achieve perfection in this task sooner than those who have not. This is the merciful miracle our Lord works, giving his grace in a special way, to the amazement of the world.

CHAPTER 31

Once you feel you have done all in your power to change your ways in accordance with the laws of the Church, this is the time to get to work on the task. And then, if you find things you have done in the past crowding into your mind between you and your God, not to mention new things and promptings of sin, you must bravely step above them with a fervent urge of love, and tread them under your feet. Then try to cover them with a thick cloud of forgetting, as though they had never been done by you or by anyone else. And if they rear up often, put them down often, as often, indeed, as they rear up. And if you find this hard work, you can look for subtle mental devices, special subterfuges, for getting rid of them: these are better learned from God through experience than from anyone in this life.

CHAPTER 32

Having said this, let me suggest something of such devices. Try them out, and find better ones, if you can.

Do all you can to behave as though you didn't know they were crowding in between you and your God. And try to look over their shoulders, as it were, as though looking for something else: this something else is God, wrapped in a cloud of unknowing. If you do this, I assure you that you will shortly find the task becoming easier. I believe that if this device is properly worked out, it is nothing other than a longing desire for God, to feel and see God as though he were here. Such a desire is charity, and should always lead to peace.

There is another device you can try if you want to. When you feel totally unable to put them down, cower down yourself under them like a coward beaten in combat, and tell yourself it is no use struggling with them any longer, and so abandon yourself to God in the hands of your enemies. Tell yourself you have been vanquished for ever. But be careful of this device, I beg you: its effect will be to make you feel "poured out like water."* But I do think that if this device is properly used, it is nothing other than knowing and feeling yourself as you are, a wretched and filthy creature, far worse than nothing: knowing and feeling this is meekness. This meekness deserves to make God himself come down in might to avenge you from your enemies, to pick you up

---

*The image is from Psalm 21:14: "I am poured out like water, and all my bones are out of joint; my heart is like wax; it is melted within my breast."

and lovingly dry the eyes of your spirit, as a father would do to his child if he saw it in mortal danger from wild boars or furious biting bears.

CHAPTER 34

If you ask me how you can embark on this task, I have to ask Almighty God to teach you himself, out of his grace and mercy, for I have to say that I cannot tell you. This is not surprising, because it is God's doing alone, especially granted to any soul he chooses, without any merit on the part of that soul. . . .

Ability to perform this task is linked to the task itself, inseparably, so that those who want to embark on it can do so, and no one else. This means that without embarking on it, a soul is as it were dead, unable to will or desire to undertake it. You have it to the extent that you will or desire it, no more and no less; yet it is not will or desire, but something you do not know that urges you to will or desire something you can never know. Don't worry if you know no more, I beg you, but keep working at it, so that you are always engaged on it.

In a nutshell: let this something work on you and lead you wherever it will. Let it be the doer, and yourself be the done to; consider it and put it aside. Do not meddle with it as though you could help it, for fear of spoiling everything. Let yourself be the wood and it the carpenter; let yourself be the house and it be the inhabitant. Be blind for a time and cut out desire for knowledge, which will be more of a hindrance than a help to you. It is enough for you to feel yourself moved by something you cannot know; all you can know is that in this movement you have no particular thought for anything below God, and that your will is directed solely Godward. . . .

CHAPTER 37

Contemplatives do not usually pray in words, but when they do, they use few—the fewer the better, really. And words of one syllable are better suited to the spiritual nature of what they are doing than longer ones. They have to keep themselves poised and watchful at the highest point of spiritual endeavour.

Let me show you what I mean through a real-life example. People terrified by sudden disaster are forced to summon all their strength, putting all their energy into one great cry for help. In such extreme situations, they are hardly going to use many words, or long ones! They will just put all force they can summon into the one word, "Help!" One short word is the best way of gaining others' attention and summoning their help.

Likewise, a short inner word, not just spoken or thought, but welling up from the depths of our being, and expressing our whole being, is clearly most efficacious. . . . So a simple prayer like this welling up from the depths of our being is going to touch Almighty God's heart more surely than any long psalm mumbled *sotto voce* without thinking what it means. This is what is meant by: "A short prayer pierces the heavens."

CHAPTER 40

Teach yourself to take in the spiritual sense of the word "sin," without distinguishing between particular sins, or between mortal and venial sins: pride, anger, envy, covetousness, sloth, gluttony or lust. What does it matter to contemplatives what sin it is, or how great a sin? They regard all sins—at least while engaged in this task—as equally great, since the slightest sin separates them from God and deprives them of spiritual peace.

Feel sin like a lump, not defining it, but equating it with yourself. And in your spirit keep crying: "Sin, sin, sin! Out, out, out!" This spiritual cry is better learned from God through experience than from any human teacher in words. It is best made purely in the spirit, without forming any particular thoughts or words. Except, that is, on the occasions when an abundance of spirit forces it into words, because your body and soul are both filled with sorrow and the burden of sin.

Deal with the short word "God" in the same way. Fill your soul with its spiritual meaning, taking no account of any of God's works—whether they are good, better or best, physical or spiritual—or of any virtue that grace may produce in a person's soul; do not try to examine whether it is meekness or charity, patience or abstinence, hope or faith, chastity or voluntary poverty. What does this matter to contemplatives? They find and experience all virtues in God, since everything is in God, as cause and effect. They believe that if they had God they would have everything, and so they do not want anything else in particular, only God who is good. You must do the same, as far as grace allows you: contemplate God wholly, and wholly God, so that nothing is at work in your mind and will except God alone.

Because for as long as you live this wretched life, you will always feel this foul stinking lump of sin in some part of you, united and congealed, as it were, in the substance of your being, alternate contemplation of these two words, "sin" and "God." Make this your general understanding: that if you had God, you would be without sin, and if you were without sin, then you would have God.

CHAPTER 43

Let nothing work in your mind or will except God. Try to crush all knowledge and sense of anything below God, treading it all hard down under the cloud of forgetting. And understand that in this task you must forget not only all beings other than yourself, and their deeds and yours, but also yourself and whatever you have done for God. A perfect lover not only loves the thing he loves more than himself, but in a way hates himself on account of the thing he loves.

Treat yourself in this way: loathe and despise everything in your mind and will except God alone. Otherwise, you can be sure, whatever it is will come between you and God. No wonder if you loathe and hate yourself, if you feel sin as a foul stinking lump, which you cannot find, but which you know is coming between you and God, a lump that is in fact yourself, since you see it as united and congealed in the substance of your being, inseparable from it, indeed.

So break down all knowledge and sense of every sort of being, but paying most attention to yourself. The way you know and sense yourself determines the way you know and sense all other beings; compared with yourself, all others are easily forgotten. If you want to prove this, you have only to realize that, once you have put all other beings and all their works—yes, even your own works!—out of your mind, you will still find, between you and your God, sheer knowledge and sense of your own existence. This knowledge and sense must always be destroyed before you can really feel your task is accomplished.

CHAPTER 46

For the love of God, go carefully about this task; don't strain your heart brutally or excessively; use desire rather than brute force. The more desire you have for the task, the meeker and more spiritual your approach will be; the more brute force you put into it, the more physical and animal-like it will be. So be careful: remember that "if an animal touches the mountain [of this task], it shall be stoned to death."* Stones are hard and dry by nature, and wound where they hit. Brute force is fastened hard in the physicality of bodily senses, and stays dry where the waters of grace run off it; it wounds the silly soul, leaving it festering in fantasies devised by demons. So beware of brute animal force; learn to love fervently but gently and demurely, physically as well as spiritually. Wait for our Lord's will politely and meekly, not snatching at it suddenly like a greedy greyhound, however much you hunger for it. Speaking playfully, I advise you to do all you can to restrain the brute urging of your soul, as though determined to do nothing to show our Lord how you long to see him, have him, feel him.

You may think this a childish and playful way of putting things, perhaps. But I reckon that those who have the grace to do and feel as I say should feel able to play wholesome games with our Lord, kissing and hugging him, as a father does with his child, so happy is he to be with it!

_____

*Heb. 12:20, citing Exod. 19: 13.

CHAPTER 49

So, I beg you, pay devout heed to this meek urge of love in your heart, and follow where it leads; it will be your guide in this life and bring you to perfect happiness in the next. It is the essence of all good living, and without it you cannot start or finish any good work. It is nothing other than a good will in accordance with God, a sort of contentment and gladness you feel in your will at all God does.

Such a good will is the essence of all perfection. All pleasures and comforts, of the body and the mind, are incidental to this, however holy they may be; they simply depend on this good will. I call them "incidental" because having them or lacking them cannot disturb the good will. This holds for this life at least: in the bliss of heaven it will not be so, since there they will be inseparably united with the essence, just as the body (in which they operate) will be with the soul. So their essence here is simply a good spiritual will. And I truly believe that those who sense the perfection of this will (as far as is possible here) will find no pleasure or comfort in this life that they would not as soon be without if such were God's will.

CHAPTER 54

Those who are engaged in this task should find that if affects their body as well their soul, making them most attractive to anyone who looks at them. Indeed, the ugliest of men or women, if grace allows them to embark on this endeavour, will find their looks suddenly changed for the better, so that those who see them will be glad of and grateful for their company, finding their spirits rejoicing and themselves helped toward God in their presence.

So seek out this gift, those of you who can get it through grace, for those who truly possess it will know how to let themselves and all that pertains to them be governed by the virtue of it. They will have the gift of discerning, when necessary, all natures and characters. They will be able to adapt themselves to all who converse with them, habitual sinners or not, without sinning themselves. All who see them will be amazed, and they will, with the help of grace, draw others to the spiritual endeavours they practise themselves.

Their faces and words will be filled with spiritual wisdom, full of fire and spirit, their discourse that of sober certainty, free from falsehood, far removed from any hypocritical pretence or pretension.

CHAPTER 67

See, my friend in the spirit, how wretched a state we have fallen into through sin! Because of this, is it any wonder that we are blindly and easily deceived in our understanding of spiritual words and deeds, especially those of us who do not yet know the faculties of our souls or how they operate?

Whenever your mind is occupied with physical matters, however good your intentions, it is operating below your proper level and leaving your soul out of it. But whenever you feel your mind occupied with the subtle nature of the faculties of your soul and how they operate in spiritual concerns, such as vices and virtues, yours or those of anyone spiritually like you in character, in order to learn to know yourself and advance your perfection, then your mind is operating within yourself and on the proper level. When, however, you find your mind occupied with nothing either physical or spiritual, but simply with the essence of God, as it is and may be seen to be if you carry out the task set out in this book, then your mind is operating above you and below your God. . . .

CHAPTER 68

In the same way, while another might tell you to gather all your faculties and wits into yourself and worship God there—well said, indeed, and nothing could be more true if properly understood!—I should not advise this, in case you take it wrongly and in a physical sense. This is what I shall tell you: take no notice of being inside yourself. And (to put it briefly) I would not have you outside yourself either, or above, or below, or behind, or on one side or the other.

"Where, then," you will ask, "can I be? Nowhere, according to you!" Quite right; that is just where I would have you. Because nowhere physically is everywhere spiritually. Take good care, then, that your spiritual endeavour be nowhere physically; you will then find that where the thing your mind is concentrating on in essence is, you are there in spirit as surely as you are in body where you are physically. And though your physical senses can find nothing to nourish them there, since they think you are doing nothing, go on doing this nothing, this precious nothing, and do it for love of God. Do not give up; work diligently on that nothing with a vigilant desire to possess God, whom no one can know. Honestly, I would rather be nowhere physically, wrestling with this blind nothing, than be such a great lord that I could be everywhere physically if I so wished, merrily playing with all this everything as a lord does with his possessions.

Let go of this everywhere and everything, for the sake of this nowhere and nothing. . . .

CHAPTER 69

A person's nature is amazingly changed through spiritual appreciation of this nothing when it happens nowhere. The first time you look at it, you find all the worst sins you have committed since your birth, physical or spiritual, secretly and darkly painted on it. However you turn it around, they still appear before your eyes, until after much hard work, heavy sighing and bitter weeping, you have largely washed them away.

In this work you will sometimes feel you are looking at hell, for you will find yourself despairing of ever achieving complete spiritual rest from such pain. Many come this far into themselves, but the great pain they feel and the lack of consolation send them back to valuing physical things, seeking outward physical relief, not finding the spiritual relief they would have found if they had persevered.

Those who persevere sometimes feel some relief, and have some hope of reaching perfection, since they feel and see that many of their earlier grievous sins have been largely rubbed out by grace.

They still feel pain, though, but see an end to it, as it steadily becomes less and less. So now they can call it nothing more than purgatory. Sometimes they can find no particular sins painted on it, but just see sin as a lump of they know not what, of nothing outside themselves; this can be called the root and pain of original sin. Sometimes they think it is paradise or heaven, because of the many wonderful delights and comforts, joys and blessed virtues they find there. Sometimes they think it is God, on account of the peace and repose they find in it.

Let them think what they will! They will always find it a cloud of unknowing between them and their God.

CHAPTER 71

Some find this business so hard and so fearsome that they say it cannot be done without an awful amount of hard work beforehand, that it can happen only rarely, and only when they are "ravished," caught up out of themselves. Let me answer this as well as my feeble powers allow, and say: all this is ordained and disposed by God, according to the spiritual ability of those to whom this gift of contemplation and spiritual striving is given.

Some cannot achieve it without long hard spiritual exercises, and can reach the fulfilment of this task only rarely and in the special call from our Lord, which is known as "ravishing." Others have such fine gifts and spirit, are so at home with God in this gift of contemplation, that they can achieve it when they want in the usual daily round: sitting, walking, standing or kneeling as the case may be. At these times they retain full control over their physical and mental faculties, and can use them if they so wish— not without some difficulty, but without any great difficulty. We have an example of the first class in Moses, and of the second in Aaron, the temple priest.

CHAPTER 74

If you think this endeavour does not agree with your physical or spiritual nature, then abandon it and take up another, taking good and reliable spiritual advice, without any blame attaching.

And then I ask you to excuse me, because I wanted to bring you benefits by this account compiled from my simple knowledge; that was what I intended. So read it through two or three times, or more: the more, the better, and so you will understand more of it. It may well be that some sentences that were difficult for you at the first or second reading will soon seem easy.

I, of course, find it impossible to understand how anyone inclined to this endeavour should read this work, silently or aloud, or hear it read, without at the time feeling it to be in full accord with the effects of that endeavour. Then, if you think it does you good, thank God with all your heart, and for the love of God, pray for me.

* * * * *

Farewell, my friend in the spirit, with God's blessing and mine! I earnestly pray to Almighty God that true peace, sound advice and spiritual comfort in God with an abundance of his gifts may be with you and all who love God on this earth. Amen.

Julian of Norwich

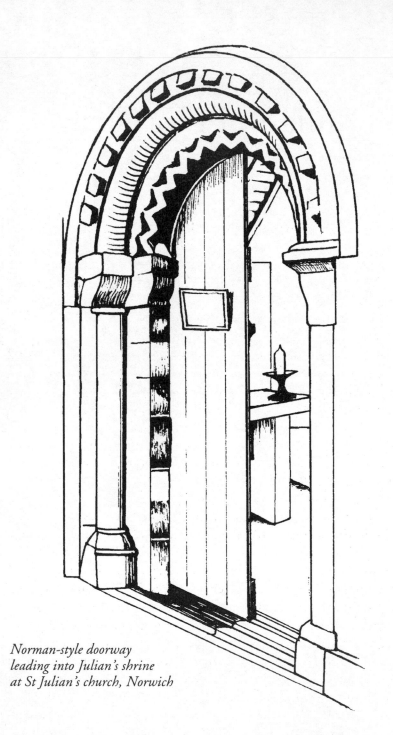

*Norman-style doorway
leading into Julian's shrine
at St Julian's church, Norwich*

JULIAN OF NORWICH

In addition to being one of the most remarkable of the English mystics, Julian of Norwich is also the first woman known to have written a book in the English language. Though the place of her birth is unknown, the year was 1342. This and a few other particulars of her life can be gleaned from her book, *The Revelations of Divine Love*, and from a handful of other contemporary documents. She was apparently a very devout woman even in her youth, deriving inspiration from, and seeking deep understanding of, the Passion of Christ. At some point in her young life she prayed for three favours from God: to be able to recall Christ's Passion; a physical illness; and to receive, as God's gift, three wounds—"the wound of true contrition, the wound of loving compassion, and the wound of longing with my will for God" (Long text, ch. 2).[1]

In the spring of her thirty-first year, Julian was stricken with a severe illness. After suffering for six days and being at the point of death, her pain suddenly abated, and she received, on 13 May 1373, from about four o'clock in the morning until the following night, sixteen revelations, or "showings," of God's love, including visions of the Passion. The revelations were experienced in a manner "most lovely and calm," but at their conclusion her pain and suffering returned and she began to think that she had merely been delirious. However, upon mentioning her visions to an attending priest, who took them quite seriously, she felt ashamed for having doubted their authenticity. By the following morning she had recovered from the ordeal, and was restored to a state "without physical illness or fear of conscience." At some point, whether it was before or after the revelations is not clear, she began her life as a solitary anchoress enclosed in a cell attached to the parish church of St Julian in Norwich (it is possible that Julian took her name from this church). She became widely known as a discerning spiritual guide, conversing with visitors through a window in her cell, and was once consulted by Margery Kempe. She apparently died there, sometime following the year 1416, after a long and deeply intense life of at least seventy-four years. No evidence remains of her place of burial.

Julian's passion was for direct experience and deep understanding of fundamental religious realities, and she arranged all her life and thought around ascertaining the meaning of the experiences she had. She composed two accounts of these revelations, a shorter version evidently written soon after their occurrence, and a longer version following twenty years of pondering their significance. Her writings are marked by vivid imagery, by a felicity of expression, by a delicacy and precision in dealing with theological insights, and by honesty and humility throughout. Her guiding themes include the "graciousness" of God, the motherhood of God (an idea revived in our own time), but primarily the depth and immensity of the love of God for his creation. After her years of searching reflection on God's meaning and purpose in the revelations, she realized simply that "love was his meaning" (Long text, ch. 86). And this was Julian's meaning as well in writing of her experience: "It is truly love which moves me to tell it to you, for I want God to be known and my fellow Christians to prosper" (Short text, ch. 6). It is an indication of her personal integrity and selflessness that she saw her rather uncommon experiences not merely as God speaking to her alone, but also as God speaking through her to the world.

As did her words through the window of her cell, Julian's writings have continued to guide and to inspire fellow Christians through the ages, especially after a modernized version of the long text was printed in 1670, and also with the publication of several versions of the short text in the present century. Concerning Julian's significance, Paul Molinari has written that "Julian helps man to look at himself with the eyes of God, and thus to experience the ultimate joy of a creature: his consciousness of being the object of his Creator's love."[2]

It is perhaps difficult for many people today, leading intensely active and secular lives, to understand the nature of or motivations for a life of solitude. But during the Middle Ages, an era very different from our own in many ways, this way of life was, if not quite popular, at least not uncommon. Solitaries were to be found not only attached to churches, but in monasteries, convents, and castles as well. During the middle of the fifteenth century, there were, at any given time, probably at least eight such persons living in Norwich. And at various times surrounding Julian's life, there were also at least eight in London, six in Winchester, others in Lincoln and York, as well as in smaller towns such as Beverley, Stafford, Hampole, Leek, Newcastle, Gainsborough, Southwell, Stamford, Dartford, and Shrewsbury. Before taking up the solitary life, the candidate would be examined by the religious authorities concerning his or her fitness for and dedication to such a life, and, following a solemn ceremony, would enter the cell and from that point onward be considered "dead unto the world and alive unto God." The cell, however, was probably more often a suite of rooms, and the isolation was, of course, not absolute. Some solitaries lived with one or two others, or in adjacent and communicating cells. Many enjoyed the company of a cat, and most apparently had maidservants to wait on them. Julian had two—Sara and Alice—during her time in Norwich. The purpose of the seclusion was, of course, to reduce external distractions and thus to facilitate the single-mindedness and inner stillness necessary for one to hear the softly-spoken Word.

The city of Norwich has been an important cosmopolitan centre for centuries. In the days of Julian it was second only to London in population and prosperity, and was located on a busy trade route for traffic to and from the Continent. Because of insanitary drainage and sewerage conditions, urban centres were especially vulnerable to the Black Death. It reached Norwich early in 1349, killing more than one third of its inhabitants, including at least one half of its resident clergy because of their frequent contact with the sick. The insidious impact of the plague seeped into every segment of society and perhaps also contributed to Julian's deep concern with the meaning of suffering and death.

Despite the disastrous effects of the plague, Norwich continued to function as a vital religious centre, with a major cathedral (operating as a Benedictine monastery), an exceptional cathedral library, three colleges of priests, and representatives of all the major religious Orders. It still boasts more medieval churches than any other city in Europe. An Augustinian friary with a substantial library stood across the road from Julian's cell during her time of residence there, and it is certainly possible that she could have been allowed to borrow spare copies of a variety of books, thus acquiring or augmenting some of the theological expertise evident in her writings.

A succession of church buildings has stood on the site of St Julian's, probably since the year 950. Though the earliest building was destroyed by invading Danes in 1004, it was rebuilt during the early decades of the eleventh century, while Canute was king of England. The Benedictine nuns of nearby Carrow Priory assumed responsibility for the church in 1135, under the author- ity of King Stephen, and it continued under their care during Julian's lifetime. At that time the church and the cell were covered by a thatched roof, and while the church maintained its integrity for several hundred more years, the cell collapsed into disrepair during the sixteenth century.

The passing centuries, however, eventually took their toll on the church itself, so much so that in 1845, with services having ceased, the building was being considered for demolition. But funds from the parishioners supported partial restoration work, which was undertaken in 1845, 1871, and 1901. Most of this work and, indeed, much of the entire structure, was destroyed during World War II, however, when a bomb hit the tower in 1942 and sent it crashing inward upon the church. The war years were, of course, a time of great loss and widespread despair. But they were also a time when Julian's *Revelations of Divine Love* was being increasingly recognized and read. This growing public interest in her life is probably what saved the church from extinc- tion and stimulated another, more thorough, restoration of both the church and the cell, according to the designs of A. J. Chaplin, work which was completed in 1953.

The history of the church and the heritage of the region are reflected in a variety of the building's features. The Saxon-style tower is presently only half its original height. The fifteenth-century bell sat outside the south wall for many years, but has now been rehung. The font is a sculptural masterpiece dating to about 1420. It originally resided in nearby All Saints Church but was brought to St Julian's in 1977, when the former church was declared redundant. It is adorned with the likenesses of twenty-four saints and apostles.

The cell now functions as a small chapel and shrine to Dame Julian. It is likely that it was occupied by other solitaries both before and after Julian's forty-some years there. The doorway into the cell would not have been there during the Middle Ages, but through the window looking out into the church Julian could view the altar, receive communion, and follow the services of worship. The stained glass in this window now carries the images of a Lily Crucifix, of Julian, and of her phrase "All shall be well," expressing the faith for which she has become so well known. It was through a small window on the opposite wall that she provided pilgrims and passers-by with comfort and counsel. At that time the view from this window would have been on to a road running along the south side of the church, and down to the River Wensum beyond.

Further details concerning the history of the building can be obtained from pamphlets available at the church, as well as from the photographs hanging in the library. Additional information on Julian's life and legacy may also be obtained there.[3] The church and the cell are open daily from 8.00 a.m. to 4.00 p.m. in winter and 8.00 a.m. to 5.30 p.m. in summer, and are located on Rouen Road, about half a mile south of Norwich Cathedral. The cathedral, by the way, contains two stained-glass windows of Julian, one in the Bauchun Chapel and the other in St Saviour's Chapel.

Notes

1. Citations, and the selections that follow, are in a version made specially for this book, with inevitable debts to modern translations. For the complete text, see: *Julian of Norwich, Showings,* trans. from the critical

text, with an Introduction by Edmund Colledge and James Walsh (New York: Paulist Press, 1978); for the Long Text only: *Julian of Norwich, The Revelation of Divine Love*, trans. with an Introduction by M. L. del Mastro (Liguori, Mo.: Triumph Books; Tunbridge Wells: Burns & Oates, 1994).

2. Paul Molinari, quoted in Clifton Wolters, "The English Mystics," in *The Study of Spirituality*, edited by Cheslyn Jones, Geoffrey Wainwright, and Edward Yarnold (Oxford and New York: Oxford University Press, 1986), p. 336.

3. In her *Julian of Norwich* (New York: Paulist Press, 1988, p. 12, n. 1), Grace Jantzen notes that at least 150 "Julian groups" meet for prayer and fellowship in Britain, and that this movement is growing in North America as well.

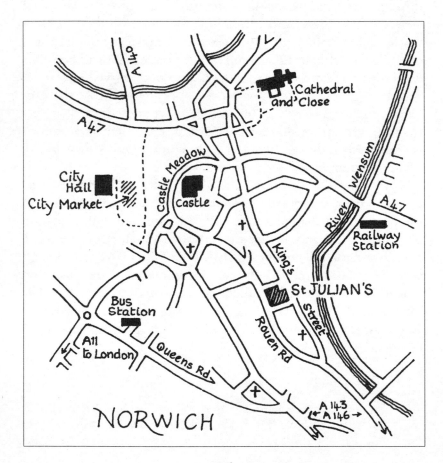

THE REVELATIONS OF DIVINE LOVE

THE SHORT TEXT: Chapter 1

Here is a vision shown by the goodness of God to a devout woman named Julian, who is a recluse in Norwich and still alive in this year of our Lord 1413. The vision contains very many words of comfort, and will be greatly moving for all those who desire to love Christ.*

I wanted three favours as gifts from God. The first was to be able to recall Christ's Passion. The second was a physical illness, and the third was to receive, as God's gift, three wounds. The first came into my mind with devotion; I seemed to have a great feeling for the Passion of Christ, but I desired to have still more by the grace of God. I wished that I had been with Mary Magdalen and the others at the time they loved Christ, so that with my own eyes I might have seen our Lord's Passion, which he suffered for me, so that I might have suffered with him as did others who loved him, even though I believed firmly in all Christ's pains, as they are shown and taught by the Church, and as paintings of the Crucifixion represent. Made by God's grace, according to the Church's teaching, they resemble Christ's Passion, insofar as human understanding can reach. But although I truly believed in them, I desired a physical sight, to give me more knowledge of our Lord and saviour's physical sufferings, and of the compassion of our Lady and of all those who truly loved him who were living at that time and saw his sufferings, for I would have been one of them and have suffered with them. I never desired any other sight of God or revelation, until my soul was separated from my body, since I really trusted that I should be saved. My intention was to gain a firmer memory of Christ's Passion from that revelation.

As to the second grace, there came into my mind, together with contrition—a free gift from God which I did not seek—a desire for God to give me a physical illness, and I wanted it to be so severe that it would seem mortal, so that in it I should receive all

---

* This brief prologue was probably added by a later commentator.

the rites the Church had to give me, whilst myself believing that I was dying, and everyone who saw me would think the same, as I wanted no comfort from any human, earthly life. In this illness I wanted to feel every kind of pain, physical and spiritual, which I would feel if I were dying, every fear of and assault from devils, and every other kind of pain except the departure of my soul, since I hoped this would profit me when I did die, because I longed soon to be with my God.

I desired these two, the revelation of the Passion and the sickness, on one condition, as neither seemed to me an ordinary petition, and so I said: "Lord, you know what I want. If it be your will for me to have it, grant it to me, and if it be not your will, good Lord, do not be displeased, for I desire nothing you do not." When I was young, I had desired to have that illness when I was thirty years old.

As to the third, I heard a churchman tell the story of St Cecilia, and from his account I gathered that she received three sword wounds in the neck, from which she died. Moved by this, I conceived a great desire, and prayed to our Lord God to grant me, during the course of my life, three wounds—the wound of contrition, the wound of compassion and the wound of longing with my will for God. While I had asked for the other two conditionally, this third I asked for without any condition. The two desires I mentioned first slipped from my mind, but the third stayed in it constantly.

THE LONG TEXT:

CHAPTER 3

The illness God sent me when I asked for it

When I was thirty-one-and-a-half years old, God sent me a physical illness, in which I lay for three days and three nights. On the fourth night I received all the rites of the Church, and I believed I would not live till morning.

After that I lay sick for two more days and nights. On the third night, I often thought I was going to die, as did those who were with me. Since I was still young, I thought it very hard to die, but not because there was anything on earth I wanted to live for, nor because I feared the pain, since I trusted in God's mercy. I rather wanted to live so that I could have loved God better, for a longer time, and so, by God's grace, have been able to know and love him better in the bliss of heaven.

All the time I had lived on earth seemed to me so insignificant and brief, compared to the reward of endless bliss, that I thought it nothing. That is why I asked: "Lord, is it possible that my living no longer is for your honour?" My reason, and all the pain I was feeling, told me I was going to die, so I gave my full assent, with all my heart and will, to being at God's disposal.

In this state I kept going till daylight, by which time my body, from the middle downward, was dead, with no feeling at all. Then I asked to be sat upright, and, with help, to be propped up, to make me feel freer in my heart to be at God's disposal, and to think about him while my life still lasted.

My curate had been sent for to be at my deathbed, but by the time he arrived my eyes had become fixed and I was unable to speak. He put a cross in front of my face and said, "I have brought you the image of your creator and saviour. Look upon it, and take comfort from it." It seemed to me that I was all right as I was, as my eyes were fixed upward, gazing up at the heaven I trusted to reach by the mercy of God. But nevertheless I agreed to fix my eyes on the face on the crucifix, if I could, and managed to do so. It seemed to me that I might last longer looking straight ahead rather than directly upward.

After this my sight started to fail, and the room around me grew as dark as if it had been night. I could see only—I don't know how—the image on the cross, in daylight. Everything other than the cross appeared ugly to me, and frightening, as if full of devils.

Then the rest of my body began to die, to the point where I had scarcely any feeling, and my most severe pain was from shortness of breath. At that point, I was sure I was going to die.

And then, suddenly, all my pain was lifted from me, and I was as whole and healthy in every part of my body as I had ever been before. I marvelled at this sudden change, as this seemed to be a secret working of God, not the work of nature. And yet this feeling of relief did not convince me that I should live, nor, in fact, was it altogether a comfort to me. For I would have preferred to be set free from this world, and had had my heart set on this.

Then I suddenly thought I ought to desire the second wound [natural compassion] as a gracious gift from our Lord, so that my body might be filled completely with understanding and experience of his blessed Passion, as I had prayed for earlier. I wanted to suffer with him, for his pain to be my pain, and after this to be completely filled with longing for him.

I felt that through his grace I might receive the wounds I had previously desired. But in this prayer I never desired any vision, or any kind of revelation from God—only the sort of compassion that, I thought, a soul following its natural inclination would have for our Lord Jesus, who out of love chose to become mortal. And so I longed to suffer with him, while living in my mortal body, as far as God's grace would allow me to.

CHAPTER 4

Beginning the first revelation, of the crowning with thorns, and how God fills the heart with the greatest joy

I suddenly saw the red blood running down from under the garland; it was hot and fresh, and just as plentiful and lifelike as though it were the time when the garland of thorns was pressed down on his blessed head, when he, who was both God and man, suffered for me. I realized with absolute conviction that it was Christ himself showing this to me, with no intermediary.

And in the same revelation, suddenly the Trinity completely filled my heart with the greatest joy. This is how, I realized, it will be in heaven, without end, for those who go there. The Trinity is God, and God is the Trinity; the Trinity is our maker and our keeper; the Trinity is our everlasting lover, our endless joy and our bliss, through our Lord Jesus Christ and in our Lord Jesus Christ. This truth was shown in the first revelation and in all of them, because where Jesus appears, there too the blessed Trinity is, in my view.

100

I exclaimed, "Bless the Lord!" in a loud voice, but meaning to be reverent. I was completely astonished, in wonder that he, who is so worthy to be revered and feared, should be so familiar and at home with a sinful creature living in this wretched flesh.

CHAPTER 10

The second revelation, of the discoloring of his face,
and of our redemption

After this I saw on the face on the crucifix that hung before me part of his Passion unfolding before my very eyes: men showing their contempt, spitting on him, sullying and buffeting him. I saw his many exhausting pains—more than I can tell—and how his face often changed colour. At one moment I saw half his face, beginning with the ear, redden over with dried blood until this covered up to the middle of his face; then the other half was covered in the same way, while in the first half the colour vanished just as it had come.

I saw this with my own eyes, though dimly and mistily, and I wanted there to be more light so that I could see it more clearly. The answer was put into my mind: "If God wants to show you more, he will be your light; you need none but him."

I was seeing him as we seek him. We are now so blind and so lacking in wisdom that we never seek God until he, out of his goodness, shows himself to us. And when we see anything of him, through his grace, we are moved by this grace to seek with a great longing to see him in a more blissful manner. So did I see him and seek him, hold him and want him—which is, and should be, the way we generally operate in this matter, I should say.

At one point, I was led in my mind down to the seashore. There I saw hills and valleys, green as though covered in moss, together with seaweed and shingle. I took this to mean that if someone were there under the wide water and given sight of God as God is continuously with us, he would be safe in soul and body and come to no harm. Furthermore, he would receive more solace and comfort than any this world may or can describe.

God wills us to believe that we see him all the time, though we seem to see him only a little, and in this belief he is constantly giving us his grace. For he wants to be seen, and to be sought; he wants us to wait for him, and to trust in him.

CHAPTER 41

The fourteenth revelation: that it is impossible to pray for mercy without receiving it; how God wants us to pray even though we are dry and barren, because that prayer is acceptable to him

Then our Lord gave me a revelation concerning prayer, in which I saw the two states in which our Lord intends us to pray. The first is righteousness, and the second is complete trust.

Our trust is still often not complete, because we are not sure that God hears us in the way we think he does, both on account of our unworthiness and because we feel absolutely nothing, since we are frequently as barren and dry after praying as before. And this folly in our feelings is the cause of our weakness, as I have felt myself.

Our Lord brought all this suddenly to my mind, and revealed these words: "I am the ground of your entreaty. First, it is my will that you should have what you ask for, and, second, I make you want it. Since I make you ask for it, which you do, how should you then not have what you ask?"

. . . .

Our Lord is most pleased and delighted with our prayer. He seeks for it, and wishes to have it, as by his grace he makes our state like his, as our nature is like his. This is his blessed will, for he says: "Pray inwardly, even if you think it is giving you no satisfaction. The prayer is profitable even if you feel nothing, even if you see nothing, even if you think you can do nothing. When you feel dry and barren, when you are sick or weak—that is when your prayer is most pleasing to me, although you find it giving you but little satisfaction. This is how it is with all your prayers made in faith, in my sight."

. . . .

CHAPTER 43

What prayer does, and how God delights in what he does for us

. . . And then, by his sweet grace, we shall, in our own humble and constant prayer, enter into him now, in this life, by many hidden touches of sweet, spiritual sights and feelings portioned out to us to the measure our simplicity can bear.

This is, and will be, carried out by the grace of the Holy Spirit, until we die longing for love. Then we shall all come home to our Lord, knowing ourselves clearly and possessing God most fully. We shall be completely possessed by God without end, seeing him in truth, feeling him in fullness, hearing him in our spirit, delectably smelling him, sweetly swallowing him. Then shall we see him face to face, in familiarity but also in fullness. Creatures, beings that are made, shall see and endlessly gaze upon God, their maker. No one can see God like this and go on living afterward— that is, in this mortal life. But when God by his special grace wills to show himself here, he strengthens creatures beyond themselves, measuring the revelation according to his will, to make it beneficial at that time.

CHAPTER 50

The soul that will be saved was never dead in the sight of God
. . . and a doubt about this

In this life mercy and forgiveness are our road, leading us evermore to grace. Judging by the storms and sorrows we, for our part, fall into, we are often dead, as we judge things here on earth. But in the sight of God the soul that will be saved was never dead and never will be.

I still wondered at this, puzzling with all my mind, and wondering in these terms: "Good Lord, I see you, truth itself, and I know in truth that we sin grievously all the time and deserve a lot of blame. Yet while I cannot escape from knowing this truth, neither do I see you putting any kind of blame on us. How can this be?"

I knew from the ordinary teaching of the Church and by my

own feelings that the blame for our sins lies continuously upon us, from the first man to the time we reach heaven. What puzzled me was this: that I saw our Lord God putting no more blame on us than if we had been as pure and holy as the angels are in heaven.

Caught in this contradiction, my reason was greatly troubled by my blindness. I could get no rest, fearing that his blessed presence might go from my sight, leaving me ignorant of how he looks on us in our sin. For either I must see in God that sin was entirely done away with, or else I ought to see in God how he sees it, which would enable me truly to know how I ought properly to see sin and how we are blamed.

CHAPTER 51

The foregoing doubt resolved by a wonderful image
of a master and a servant

Then our gracious Lord resolved my doubt by giving me most sweetly a wonderful image of a master who had a servant, and helped me to understand both. The image was presented in two forms for both the master and the servant. The first form was spiritual, but with a physical image. The second was more spiritual, without a physical image.

In the first part I saw two physical images of persons, of a master and a servant, and with these images God gave me spiritual understanding. The master sat solemnly, resting and at peace. The servant stood in front of his master in a reverent posture, ready to do his master's will.

The master looked most fondly, sweetly and gently at his servant. He sent him to a certain place to do what he asked. The servant did not just go: out of love, he jumped up suddenly and ran in great haste to carry out what his master had asked. Whereupon he fell into a ravine and was very seriously injured. He groaned and moaned, twisted and turned, but he could not get up or help himself in any way.

In all this the greatest danger was his lack of comfort, for he could not turn his face to look up to his loving master, who was very close to him and could provide complete comfort. But feebly and foolishly, he concentrated, for the moment, on his hurts and remained in distress.

In this plight he suffered seven great pains. The first was the severe bruising sustained in his fall, which made him feel great pain. The second was caused by the weight of his body. The third was the weakness that resulted from the first two. The fourth was that his mind was blinded and stunned, to the extent that he had almost forgotten the love he felt for his master. The fifth was that he could not get up. The sixth pain was the most surprising to me, and that was that he lay alone. I looked all round me and peered far and near, high and low, but I could see no help for him. The seventh pain was that the ravine in which he was lying was long, hard and rough.

I wondered at the fact that this servant could suffer his plight there so meekly. And I looked attentively to see if I could discover any fault in him, or if the master was blaming him for anything. In fact, I could find no fault, as the only reason for his fall was his good will and his great haste, and he was still as zealous, and as willing, and as inwardly good, as when he had stood in front of his master ready to do what was asked of him.

His loving master looked at him continually in just this way, with a twofold expression. The first part was outward. It was most gentle and kind, full of compassion and pity. The second part was inward. It was more spiritual. This was shown by my spirit's being led into the master; this enabled me to see him rejoice greatly, because of the glorious and noble raising he was proposing to bring to his servant through his abundant grace. (All this refers to the second part of the image.)

Now my mind was drawn back to the first part of the image, while keeping both in mind. Then our gracious Lord told me what he meant us to understand: "Look! Look at my beloved servant! See what harm and pains he has suffered in my service, for my love. Yes, and because of the good will he showed, is it not reasonable that I should reward him for his fright and his dread, his pains and his injuries, and all his distress? Not only this, but must I not give him a reward that will be better for him and give him greater honour than simply restoring him to physical health? Otherwise, it seems to me that I will have done him no favour."

With this, my soul received an inward spiritual revelation of what the Lord meant. In it I saw that it ought and indeed had to be, given the Lord's great goodness and glory, that his most precious servant, whom he loved so much, should indeed be nobly and blissfully rewarded for ever, beyond what he would have received if he had not fallen—so much so that his falling and all the distress he suffered from it should be turned into exalted, surpassing glory and everlasting bliss.

CHAPTER 54

We should be glad that God lives in our soul and our soul in God

Because of God's great and everlasting love for all humankind, he makes no distinction in love between the blessed soul of Christ and the least of the souls that will be saved. It is very easy to believe that the blessed soul of Christ lives entirely in heaven, in the glorious godhead. And in fact, as I understood what our Lord meant, where the blessed soul of Christ is, there is the substance of all the souls that will be saved by Christ. We should rejoice greatly that God lives in our soul, with a far greater presence than that of our soul in God. Our soul is made to be God's dwelling place, and the dwelling place of our soul is God, who is uncreated. It is an exalted realization inwardly to see and know that God, who is our maker, lives in our soul, and a still more exalted realization to see and to know in our mind that our soul, which is created, lives in God's substance. By this substance and made so by God, we are what we are.

CHAPTERS 59 AND 60

God as our Mother

Just as God is truly our Father, so he is truly our Mother. He revealed this truth in everything, but especially in those sweet words, "I am it!"—that is to say, "I am the strength and the goodness of fatherhood. I am it—the insight and nature of motherhood. I am it—the light and grace that is all-blessed love. I am it—the Trinity. I am it—the unity. I am it—the sovereign goodness of every kind of thing. I am it—what makes you long and love. I am it—the everlasting fulfillment of all true desires!"

Where the soul is most exalted, noble and full of praise, there is it lowest, most humble and gentle.

. . . .

I understand three ways of looking at motherhood in God. The first is that he is the ground of our natural generation. The second is how he takes our nature, where the motherhood of grace begins. The third is his motherhood in his actions. In these three, there is a spreading-out, far and wide, high and low, of the one grace without end. And all is one love—his own.

The properties of motherhood are natural love, wisdom and knowledge—and this is God. For though it is true that our physical birth is a small thing, low and simple, compared to our spiritual birth, it is God who does the mothering through the creatures from whom we are born.

A natural loving mother, who recognizes and knows the needs of her child, cares for it most tenderly, as is in the nature of motherhood to do. She continually, as the child grows in age and size, changes what she does, but her love remains the same. When the child has grown older, she allows it to be corrected, breaking down the child's vices to enable it to receive virtues and grace.

It is our Lord doing this work, with all that is fair and good, through those who do it. In this way he is our Mother in nature, through the working of grace in the lower part of our nature for love of the higher. And he wills us to know it, since he wills to have all our love fixed on him.

By seeing these things, I understood that all the debts we owe, according to God's commandment, to fatherhood and motherhood, are repaid by our truly loving God for his Fatherhood and Motherhood. Christ brings this blessed love about in us. This was revealed in everything, especially in the fine, generous words, "I am what you love."

The sixteenth revelation, a conclusion to and confirmation of the previous fifteen, though I said I had hallucinated in my sickness; how I saw the soul, and knew that it was Jesus who showed me all this

After this, the good Lord gave me the sixteenth revelation, on the following night. This was the conclusion to and confirmation of the preceding fifteen.

But first I must tell you how weak, wretched and blind I was. I said at the beginning, "And then, suddenly, all my pain was taken from me." This pain caused me no grief and no discomfort as long as the fifteen revelations continued. At the end of them, everything was closed and I saw no more. Soon I felt that I would live and suffer longer, and my sickness immediately returned, first in my head, with a loud noise. Suddenly my entire body was completely filled with sickness, just as it had been before, and I was as barren and dry as if I had never had any comfort. Like a coward, I mourned in depression brought on by my physical pains and the absence of spiritual and physical comfort.

Then a person in religion came and asked me how I was progressing. I said I had hallucinated, and he laughed aloud and inwardly. Then I said that the cross that stood in front of me seemed to bleed a great deal. At this, the person I was speaking to became very serious and was amazed.

Immediately, I was very ashamed and astonished that I could be so reckless. I thought, "This man, who never saw any of it himself, takes the least word I say seriously." And when I saw that he accepted it so seriously and with such great reverence, I wept and was deeply ashamed of my own unbelief. I wanted to be absolved in confession, but at that point I couldn't tell it to any priest, for I thought: "How can a priest believe me when I do not believe our Lord God—as I showed when I said I had hallucinated?"

Despite the fact that I really believed him while I saw him, and that I was determined then to continue to do so forever, neverthe-less, like a fool, I let the reality pass out of my mind. See what a wretch I was! It was a great sin and a most unnatural thing for me, because of the trifle of feeling a little physical pain, to have so foolishly abandoned, for the moment, the comfort of all this blessed revelation from our Lord God.

This shows you what I am in myself. But our gracious Lord would not leave me to myself. I lay still until night, trusting in his mercy, and then I fell asleep.

. . . .

Then our good Lord opened the eye of my spirit and showed me my soul in the middle of my heart. I saw the soul as large as if it were a world without end and also as if it were a blessed, blissful kingdom. Through this revelation, I understood that the soul is a glorious city.

. . . .

Jesus will never ever, as I see it, remove himself from the place he occupies in our soul. For his most natural home and his eternal dwelling is in us. He showed this in the delight he takes in the creation of our soul. For just as the Father and the Son made creatures, so did the Holy Spirit will that our soul should be made—and so it was done. Therefore, the blessed Trinity rejoices without end in the creation of our soul, for God saw without beginning what would please him without end.

. . . .

This was a delectable and restful revelation, and this is how it will be without end. The contemplation of this reality while we are here is most pleasing to God and most beneficial to us. The soul that contemplates it in this way makes itself like the One who is contemplated, and joins itself to him in rest and peace by his grace.

. . . He reassured me that it was in fact he who had shown me everything before this. When I had gazed attentively at what was being shown, our good Lord showed me words, very gently, without any sound and without opening his lips, just as he had done before, and said most sweetly: "Now know well that it was no hallucination you had today, but accept it, believe it, keep yourself in it, comfort yourself with it, and trust in it, and you will not be overcome."

. . . .

Ever since these revelations, I have longed to know what our Lord meant. It was more than fifteen years after they took place that I heard a voice in my mind, saying: "So you want to know what our Lord meant? You can be sure that what he meant was love. And who revealed it to you? Love himself. Why did he reveal it to you? For love. Hold on to this and you will know more about love, but about nothing else—ever."

Margery Kempe

Misericord showing the head of the Black Prince, in the choir of St Margaret's Church, which Margery Kempe would have known, as she lay on the floor nearby and wept

MARGERY KEMPE

While most of the English mystics represented in these pages pursued some form of an essentially solitary life in order to cultivate their spiritual sensitivity, Margery Kempe lived out her spirituality immersed in the drama of fourteenth-century family and community life. With her the ideas and advice of the hermitage and cell are brought into the marketplace, the kitchen, and the pilgrim's rugged road. She was much less a spiritual director than a dedicated disciple, and the experiences recorded in her autobiographical *Book* enable the modern reader to tread sympathetically with her the often difficult path of feminine spirituality through the late medieval world.

Margery Kempe was born about 1373 in Bishop's Lynn, a bustling port in the county of Norfolk, whose name was changed to King's Lynn in 1537. Though nothing is known of her mother, Margery's father was an important figure in the town, having been mayor five times and member of parliament six times. In 1393, at about the age of twenty, Margery was married to John Kempe, a devout and compassionate man who apparently worked as a brewer and also served as a municipal official.

Margery's *Book*, the first autobiography in the English language, contains no account of her childhood, but begins, rather, with the difficult pregnancy and *postpartum* emotional crisis surrounding the birth of her first child. She recounts that she became insane and "was prodigiously plagued and tormented by spirits for half a year, eight weeks and a few days" (ch. 1).[1] She was released from this trauma upon having a vision of Christ "looking at me with so much holiness in his face that I felt myself inwardly fortified."

After her inspired recovery from this harrowing illness, Margery's attention was nudged in the direction of the spiritual life, but she was nevertheless unable to give up her habits of pride and ostentatious dressing, fuelled by her consuming desire for status and respect. This same desire led her to establish her own brewery, which flourished for three or four years and then failed badly, as well as a milling business, which suffered the same fate. It then became rumoured that she might be in some way cursed, but she interpreted these adversities as a divine call away from her selfish concerns to a larger life in the Spirit, a life she then, wholeheartedly, decided to pursue.

The outer turning of Margery's life was soon met with a true inner conversion. One night as she lay in bed she heard, as she describes it, "a melodious sound that was so sweet and lovely I thought that I must be in paradise. So straightaway I jumped out of bed saying, 'What a shame that I ever sinned! It's so joyful in heaven!'" (ch. 3). The memory of this sublime symphony, which, as Richard Rolle would certainly appreciate, surpassed without comparison any earthly melody, remained with Margery for the rest of her life. It transformed her perception of the world and initiated a tendency toward uncontrollable weeping and an almost irresistible impulse to speak of heavenly things, the two traits that became her most distinctive characteristics and that would bring both comfort and concern to her and others in the years to come.

Margery then set out to focus her energies ever more firmly on spiritual things. She sought the counsel of priests, hermits, and anchorites, including Julian of Norwich, throughout England, and undertook more extensive and often arduous pilgrimages to the Continent and, in 1413, to Jerusalem. Also in this year she was successful in persuading her husband, after some twenty years of marriage and fourteen children, to enter with her into a vow of chastity, an arrangement that she felt would allow her to cleave more fully and freely to God. These and many more dramatic, colourful, and intimate episodes and spiritual experiences are included in her *Book*, which she, being unable to read or write, dictated to two scribes, beginning around 1431. She died in the town of her birth sometime after 1438.

Margery Kempe's *Book* reveals a rich and apparently quite accurate memory for events, especially conversations, which occurred over a span of about forty years. Margery was also familiar with the Bible, through the willingness of a young priest to read to her, and with some of the contemporary classics of spiritual direction, including Rolle's *Fire of Love* and Hilton's *Scale of Perfection.*

What is more significant than her power of memory, however, is her ability for recollection in a deeper sense, for what Martin Thornton calls "the symbolic interpretation of the created world," in which "every creature and every human situation encountered in daily life spontaneously carries a symbolic reference to some aspect of the Gospel story."[2] Margery's burning desire was, as was Julian's, to participate in the life of Christ. Through her meditation on gospel images and episodes, the elements of this story came to interpenetrate her everyday life, so that eventually her thoughts were so united with God that she never forgot him, and having him constantly in mind she perceived him in all created things (ch. 72). This habit of recollection, a standard element of traditional devotional practice, enabled Margery to read a transcendent meaning and presence in the most common events in the book of the created world through a special, heartfelt identification with the Author.

As a devout woman in the late Middle Ages, Margery Kempe both benefitted from and contributed to a growing tradition of feminine spirituality. Since the middle of the thirteenth century, holy women were increasing in number and influence and while many pursued the path of the convent or the solitary cell, others, who Clarissa Atkinson says were a new creation of that age, lived out their vocation in the more complicated context of family and community life.[3] These sincere spirits, being women, were barred from acquiring the religious authority derived from theological training or official church positions. Instead, they cultivated the more available and immediate authority of mystical experience.

Margery suffered much public ridicule for her particular habits and general lifestyle following her conversion, but the understanding and support she did sometimes receive were certainly due, at least in part, to the widespread knowledge of other saintly women, who, along with their male counterparts, were the celebrities of the Middle Ages. Evidently the only holy woman with whom Margery was personally acquainted was Julian of Norwich, whose wise counsel is recorded in Chapter 18 of her *Book*. But she was also familiar with the lives and legends of several others, and mentions in her *Book* St Bridget of Sweden, Mary of Oignies, who also, like Margery, had the "gift of holy tears," and St Elizabeth of Hungary. Her sense of solidarity with these active and outspoken women, a feeling built on her hearing of their stories from books and pulpits, fortified her on her pilgrimage from an ambitious businesswoman and housewife of Lynn to a mystical inhabitant of the long-hidden Holy Land.

It seems especially appropriate that the parish church where Margery Kempe worshipped was dedicated to St Margaret of Antioch, who was considered the special protectress of women in labour. This church, the full name of which is the Priory Church of St Margaret with St Mary Magdalene and all the Virgin Saints, was founded in 1101 by Herbert de Losinga, bishop of Norwich, and was associated with the adjacent Benedictine priory. Two Norman towers were added at the west end of the small original building around 1150, but by the thirteenth century most of this building and much of the towers had been demolished to make way for a new and much larger structure some 235 feet in length.

Margery was well known at St Margaret's during the early fifteenth century, being actively involved in both the spiritual and social life of the church, but many parishioners were not exactly sure what to make of her. In chapter 9 of her *Book*, Margery says that once on a Friday before Whitsunday, when she was kneeling in the church hearing Mass, a stone and part of a beam fell from the highest part of the vault onto her head and back with such weight that she thought her back would be broken or even that she would die. But she soon asked God for mercy and immediately her pain was gone and she became "entirely well and in one piece." A Carmelite friar named Master Aleyn, a native of Lynn and a friend to Margery, investigated the event and upon weighing the three-pound stone and the six-pound beam, declared her survival a miracle. Many people agreed with the friar's assessment, but as a whole the townspeople remained divided on the interpretation of the event—was it a sign of divine mercy that she was not injured or killed, or a sign of divine displeasure that it happened at all?

Although Margery's habitual weeping and wailing were severely criticized by many parishioners, her tears were welcomed and even encouraged by all on at least one day early in 1421. On a bright, clear January day a great fire consumed the Guildhall of the Holy Trinity, situated just across the market-place from the church, and threatened to burn St Margaret's and, indeed, the entire town. As Margery recounts in chapter 67, the townspeople begged her to continue crying and praying for divine mercy on the town, and as she sat in the church weeping and sadly watching sparks from the fire enter the roof through the lantern, three men came to her with snow on their clothes saying that her prayers had been answered by the sudden arrival of a snowstorm. While the people of Lynn were grateful to Margery for what they saw as a rather miraculous event, when the crisis was past they soon resumed their critical ways. Over the years, though, she was sometimes consulted for her divine intuitions concerning various practical affairs of the church and community.

Twenty years earlier another unfortunate fire had touched the life of the church. At that time William Sawtrey was parish priest of St Margaret's, and when Parliament passed the statute *De haeretico comburendo* (On the burning of the heretic) in 1401, he, being a Lollard, was accused of heresy and became the statute's first victim, burned in chains at Smithfield. Margery, who probably knew Sawtrey, was herself suspected several times of Lollardry and other heretical ideas, but upon repeated examination before Church authorities was always able to demonstrate her orthodoxy.

By 1453 the north-west tower of the church had been rebuilt, this time in Perpendicular Style, its foundations having slowly given way over the passing centuries. A high pointed spire was added to the top of the south-west tower, but at noon on 8 September 1741 a violent storm sent this spire crashing down into the church, destroying much of the nave. Within three years a new Georgian Gothic nave had been constructed, along with new transepts, thus establishing many of the major contours of the building as it stands today.

Upon entering the church through the main west door, evidence of the infirm foundations of the original north-west tower can be seen in the leaning stonework on the left. Farther up along the left-hand side of the nave is the early Georgian pulpit, which is adorned with inlaid panels and canopy. Just beyond the pulpit is the organ, which was designed by organist Dr Charles Burney (father of Fanny and friend of Mozart) and built in 1754. The screens at the back of the chancel are from the fourteenth and fifteenth centuries and display some fine carving, including the Black Prince and his "shield of peace," which Margery would have known.

In the aisle on the south side, opposite the organ, are the two largest brasses in England. One dates to 1349 and is the work of Adam de Walsoken. The other was done in 1364 by Robert Braunche and depicts his wife's dog and a peacock feast he gave for King Edward III.

The colourful seventeenth-century moon clock on the outside of the south-west tower serves as a reminder that the fortunes of the town through the ages have depended in large part on the ebb and flow of the Great Ouse river. The letters around the perimeter of the clock are each two hours apart and spell "Lynn High Tide," with the revolving central disc showing the phases of the moon and the dragon of St Margaret indicating the times of the daily high tides. High water marks during several floods can also be seen near the base of this tower.

Beyond the walls of St Margaret's, along Priory Lane, lie the remains of the fourteenth-century Benedictine monastery, part of which has been restored and converted into private residences. At various times, beginning in the thirteenth century, there have also been Augustinian, Carmelite, Dominican, and Franciscan monasteries in Lynn. Across the street to the north of the church is Trinity Guildhall, where the snow once quenched a fire, and beyond it a town with numerous buildings of historical and architectural interest.

King's Lynn is located in East Anglia, just inland from The Wash, which, when the town was chartered in 1204, extended almost to the edge of this soon-to-be-substantial seaport. It can be reached by a number of major roads and is at the terminus of the railway line from London through Cambridge and Ely. It can also be reached by rail from London via the main East Coast line from King's Cross, changing at Peterborough.

Notes

1. Quotations from Margery's *Book* and the extracts that follow are taken from *The Book of Margery Kempe*, in a new translation by Tony D. Triggs (Tunbridge Wells: Burns & Oates; Old Brookville, N.Y.: Triumph Books, 1995).

2. Martin Thornton, *English Spirituality* (London: SPCK, 1963. Reprint, with new Preface, New York: Cowley, 1986), pp. 223-4.

3. Clarissa W. Atkinson, *Mystic and Pilgrim: The Book and the World of Margery Kempe* (Ithaca, N.Y.: Cornell University Press, 1983), ch. 6.

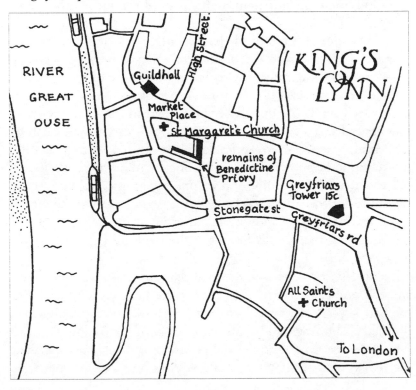

THE BOOK OF MARGERY KEMPE

At the start of her book, Margery Kempe describes her early vicissitudes and the call of God

When I was twenty, or a little older, I was married to a well-respected burgess, and things being what they are I quickly found myself pregnant. During the pregnancy and up to the time the child was born I suffered from severe attacks of illness; and then, what with the labour of giving birth on top of my previous illness, I despaired of my life and thought that I would not survive.

At that point I sent for my priest, because I had something on my conscience which I had never before divulged in my life. For I was constantly hindered by my enemy, the devil, who was always telling me that so long as I was in good health I had no need to make confession; I should just do penance by myself, in private, and God, in his all-sufficient mercy, would forgive me for everything.

And therefore I often did harsh penances, restricting myself to bread and water; I also did other godly deeds, praying devoutly but never revealing my guilty secret in the course of confession.

But when I was ever sick or out of spirits, the devil whispered to me that I would be damned because I had not been absolved of that special sin. Therefore, not expecting to survive the birth of my child, I sent for my priest, as I've already told you, fully intending to be absolved for everything I had done in my life.

But when I was on point of revealing my long-concealed secret, my confessor was a little too hasty with me; he began to tell me off in no uncertain terms, before I had even covered all I meant to say; and after that, try as he might, he couldn't get me to say a word.

Eventually, what with my fear of damnation on the one hand and the priest's sharp tongue on the other, I became insane, and for half a year, eight weeks and a few days I was prodigiously plagued and tormented by spirits.

During that time I saw (or believed I saw) devils opening their mouths as if to swallow me, and revealing waves of fire that were burning inside their bodies. Sometimes they grabbed at me, sometimes they threatened me; they tugged and pulled me, night and day for the whole eight months. They also bayed at me fearsomely, and told me to forsake the Church and its faith and deny my God, his Mother and all the saints in heaven.

They told me to deny my good works and all my good qualities, and turn my back on my father, my mother and all my friends. And that's what I did: I slandered my husband, my friends and my own self. I said many wicked and cruel things; I was empty of any virtue or goodness; I was bent on every wickedness; I said and did whatever the spirits tempted me to say and do. At their instigation I would have destroyed myself many times over and been damned with them in Hell; and as if to show determination I bit my own hand so savagely that the mark has been visible ever since.

What's more, I used my nails (for I had no other instrument) to scratch myself viciously, ripping the skin on my chest near my heart. And if I'd had my own way I would have done even more to myself, but I was bound and restrained by force day and night. I suffered from these and other temptations for such a long while that people thought I'd never recover or even survive, but then something happened: as I lay by myself, without my attendants, our merciful Lord Jesus Christ—ever to be trusted! his name be praised!—never forsaking his servant in a time of need, appeared to me—his creature who had forsaken him—in human form, the most pleasing, most beautiful, loveliest sight that human eyes could ever behold. Dressed in a mantle of purple silk, he sat by the bed, looking at me with so much holiness in his face that I felt myself inwardly fortified. And he spoke to me in the following way: "Daughter, why have you abandoned me, when I never thought to abandon you?"

And instantly, as he spoke these words, I swear that I saw the air open up as brightly as any shaft of lightning. And he rose up into the air, not very fast or quickly but with grace and ease, so that I could clearly see him in the air until it closed again.

And at once my composure and mental faculties came back to me, just as they had been before, and I begged my husband, as soon as he came, for the keys of the cellar so that I could get myself food and drink as I had done in the past. My maids and attendants advised him not to hand over any keys; they said I would only give away such stores as we had, for they thought that I was beside myself.

Nevertheless, my husband, who was always kind and sympathetic to me, ordered them to give me the keys; and I got myself food and drink, insofar as my physical health would allow me to do so. And I recognized my friends, the members of my household and all the others who came to see the act of mercy which our Lord Jesus Christ had performed upon me. Blessed may he be, who is always close to us in our troubles. When people think he is far away he is right beside them, full of grace.

Afterwards, I returned to all my other household duties, doing everything in a quite level-headed and sober way but not really knowing the call of our Lord.

When, mercifully, I had thus returned to my right mind, I fancied that I was bound to God and would be his servant. However, neither my husband nor anyone else could persuade me to give up being vain or enjoying the trappings of wealth I was used to. Yet I knew very well that people said some very unpleasant things about me, for I wore gold braid in my hair, and my hoods and tippets were slashed [to show the silken linings]. As for my cloaks, the fabric was cut so that the pieces of various colours could be sewn in place, thus attracting men's eyes and gaining ever more adulation for myself.

And when my husband told me to stop being proud he got a short, sharp answer. I said I had come from a good family—too good for him to have married into—for my father had been Mayor of Lynn and afterwards the alderman of the town's Holy Guild of the Trinity; so I meant to keep my family's respect whatever people might say about me.

My neighbours were very jealous of me, and wished that they were as well-dressed as I was. My only wish was to be admired. I would not take correction, and unlike my husband I wasn't content with the things God gave me; I always wanted more than I had.

Then out of sheer greed I began to brew ale, and for three or four years I was one of the leading brewers in Lynn. In the end, though, I lost a great deal of money, for I lacked experience in the trade. I had excellent servants who knew a lot about brewing ale, yet they never seemed to get it quite right. The ale foamed up as well as anyone could wish—but then the foam disappeared and the ale went to waste. This affected batch after batch, and my servants felt so bad that they left.

Then I remembered how God had punished me before—not that I had heeded it. Now he was punishing me again by taking away my goods. So I gave up and did not brew any more.

Then I asked my husband to forgive me because I had not followed his advice sooner. I said that my pride and sinfulness were the reason for all these punishments, and resolved to lead a better life, though I'd acted with the best of intentions.

Yet I did not entirely renounce worldly things, for I turned my mind to a new line of business. I had a mill that was powered by horses, so I got two good horses and a servant, and reckoned on earning my living by grinding people's corn. This enterprise did not last long, for shortly afterwards, on the eve of the feast of Corpus Christi, a miracle happened.

The servant was in good physical health and both the horses were sturdy and reliable, having always worked the machinery well. Now on this occasion the man took one of the horses and put it in the mill as usual, but the horse refused to pull, no matter what the man did. The man was upset and racked his brains as to how he could get the horse to pull. Sometimes he led him by the head, sometimes he beat him, sometimes he coaxed him. Nothing worked, for the horse would rather go backwards than forwards. Then the man put a sharp pair of spurs on his heels and got up onto the horse's back to make him pull, but to no avail.

When the man realized how hopeless it was, he put the horse back in the stable and gave him corn, and he ate well, with a good appetite. And later he took the other horse and put him in the mill, and this horse behaved like its partner had done before, for nothing the man did would make him pull. Then the man gave up his job and would not remain with me any longer. It was soon being said round the town of Lynn that neither man nor beast would give me service.

Then some people said that I was cursed or that God was taking vengeance on me for all to see. Some said one thing and some said another. Some wise men, whose thinking reflected their love of our Lord, said that our Lord Jesus Christ was showing his ineffable mercy by calling me from the pride and vanity of the wretched world.

Then I decided that all these troubles besetting me on every side were the scourges by which our Lord would punish my sinfulness. Asking God's mercy, I renounced my pride, my greed and my love of worldly renown. I mortified my body and set out on the path to everlasting life, as I mean to explain in the pages that follow.

One night, as I lay in bed with my husband, I heard a melodious sound that was so sweet and lovely I thought that I must be in Paradise. So straight away I jumped out of bed saying, "What a shame that I ever sinned! It's so joyful in heaven!" This melody was so sweet that it surpassed all the melody that anyone could hear in this world; there was no comparison. And so, after that, whenever I heard any music or revelry I wept profusely, shedding copious tears of deep devotion, sobbing and sighing for the bliss of heaven without a thought for the shame and despite of this wretched world.

And always, after this holy call, I kept the joy and the melody of heaven in my mind—so much so that I could hardly stop myself speaking about it. For when I was in company I would often say, "It's so joyful in heaven!" And those who knew how I'd lived beforehand and now heard me saying so much about the joys of heaven said to me, "Why are you always talking about the joy of Heaven? You don't know what it's like; you haven't been there any more than us!" And they were angry with me because I wouldn't (like them) either hear or speak about worldly things, though I had done before.

And from this time onwards I never wanted sexual intercourse with my husband, for this matrimonial duty was so loathsome to me that I felt that I would rather eat or drink the oozing slime in the gutter than consent to any physical relationship (except on my obedience). So I said to my husband, "It isn't for me to deny you my body, but my heart and my feelings are drawn away from all earthly things and devoted to God." He insisted on having his own way and I let him do so, but I was full of tears and sorrow because I couldn't live my life chastely. And I frequently asked my husband to live a life of sexual abstinence, and I said that I was very conscious of how we had often displeased God by our passionate love and the high degree of sensual pleasure we had had from each other, so by common desire and common consent we should now deliberately punish ourselves and mend our ways by refusing to serve our bodily lust. My husband said it was right to do so, but not just yet—he would do so when it was God's will. And so he availed himself of me as he had done before; he wouldn't desist. And all the time I prayed to God to let me live chastely, and three or four years later, when it pleased our Lord, he made a vow of chastity, as I shall later recount if Jesus gives me leave to do so.

On her pilgrimage to Jerusalem Margery Kempe is ostracised by her fellow pilgrims, and for part of the trek she has only an elderly man to help her find her way

I left feeling thoroughly sad and miserable. I was particularly upset because I was in a foreign country, and neither I nor my guide knew a word of the language. And so we went on our way together in considerable fear and unhappiness. And on the road, the man said to me, "I am scared that you'll be abducted, and that because of you I'll be beaten up and robbed of my coat."

I replied, "William, don't be afraid. God will look after us really well." And every day I remembered the gospel story about the woman who was taken in adultery and brought before our Lord. And as I called it to mind I prayed, "Lord, as you drove away her enemies so drive away mine, and preserve my chastity which I have dedicated to you; may I never be defiled, for if I am, Lord, I vow that I shall never return to England for as long as I live."

And so we went on our way each day and met all sorts of

friendly people, and they didn't say anything offensive to me but gave me and my companion food and drink; and in many places where we called, the good wives at inns let me share their beds out of love for God.

And as I travelled, our Lord gave me the great blessing of an untroubled spirit. And so God brought me all the way to Bologna.

And after my arrival, who should turn up but the companions who had previously left me behind? They were amazed when they heard that I had got to Bologna before them, and one of their number came and begged me to go and see if they would let me rejoin their fellowship, and that's what I did. [And they said to me,] "If you want to travel as one of us you must make a new agreement with us: that you won't keep on about the Gospel in all our stopping places, but will sit there and enjoy yourself at mealtimes like the rest of us." I agreed to this and they let me join their company again. Then they moved on to Venice, and they stayed there for thirteen weeks. And every Sunday I took communion in a large house of nuns, who treated me very hospitably. And when I was there our merciful Lord Jesus Christ used to overcome me with deep devotion and copious tears, to the great amazement of the ladies who lived there.

And some time later, as I sat eating with my travelling companions, I quoted gospel texts that I had learned in the past along with other useful words. And straight away my companions said I had broken my promise. And I replied "Yes, sirs, the fact is that I can no longer keep my agreement with you. I cannot help speaking of my Lord Jesus Christ, even if the whole world forbids me to do so."

Then I took to my room and ate alone for six weeks, until our Lord made me so ill that I thought myself as good as dead, only for the Lord to suddenly make me well again. And my maid left me by myself the whole time, preferring to prepare the company's food and wash their clothes than to lift a finger for me—the mistress she had promised to serve.

This company which had excluded me from their table so that I could no longer eat with them engaged a ship to carry them [to the Holy Land]. They bought containers for their wine and organized bedding for themselves but nothing for me. Seeing their unkindness, I went to the same supplier as them, and provided myself with bedding just as they had done. And I went where they were and showed them what I had done, intending to sail with them in the ship they had hired.

Afterwards, when I was thinking things over, our Lord spoke to me inwardly and warned me not to sail in that ship, and he chose a different ship for my voyage—a galley, in fact. I told some of the company about it and they passed it on to all the rest, and as a result they didn't dare to put to sea in the ship which they had arranged for themselves. So they sold the containers they had got for their wine and fell over themselves to get on board the galley where I was. And so, much against my wishes, they became my fellow passengers, for they didn't dare do otherwise.

When it was time to make their beds they locked up my bed clothes, and a priest who was in the party took one of my sheets and said it was his. I took God as my witness that it was mine. Then the priest swore a great oath. By the Bible in his hand I was an out-and-out liar, to be despised and condemned. And so I suffered endless torment until I reached Jerusalem. And before I arrived there I spoke to those who I thought had some sort of grievance against me. "I beg you, sirs," I said to them, "be on good terms with me just as I am with you, and forgive me for having upset you on the journey. And if any of you have wronged me at all, I forgive you for it—and may God forgive you too."

And so we proceeded into the Holy Land until we could see Jerusalem. And when I saw it—riding, as I was, on the back of an ass—I thanked God with all my heart; and I prayed that just as he had brought me to see this earthly city of Jerusalem so, of his mercy, he would give me the grace to see the city of Jerusalem on high—the city of heaven. Our Lord Jesus Christ, responding to the thought that had passed through my mind, said that I would have my desire. Communing with the Lord brought me such a feeling of joy and sweetness that I was on the point of falling from my ass, for the God-given sweetness and grace in my soul were too much to bear. Then two German pilgrims came to me and saved me from falling. One was a priest, and he put spices in my mouth to make me better, for he thought I was ill. And so they helped me into Jerusalem.

And when I arrived, I said, "Sirs, I beg you not to be annoyed if I weep bitter tears in this holy place where Jesus Christ our Lord lived and died." Then we went to the temple in Jerusalem, and we were let in that day at the time for saying evensong, and we stayed there until the time for saying evensong on the following day. Then the friars lifted up a cross and led the pilgrims from place to place to see where Christ had suffered the torments of his passion, and every man and woman carried a wax candle. All the while, as we went about, the friars explained what our Lord had endured at every point. And I wept and sobbed as profusely as if I could see our Lord before my very eyes, suffering his passion there and then.

And by using my imagination I could see him clearly in my mind's eye, standing before me, and so I shared in his suffering. And when we ascended onto the mount of Calvary I couldn't stand or kneel but fell down. My body writhed and tossed about, I flung my arms wide and cried out as though my heart would burst, for in the city of my soul I saw the stark truth of our Lord's crucifixion. Right in front of my face I heard and saw with my inner perception the grief of our Lady, St John, Mary Magdalene, and many others who loved our Lord. And I had such great compassion and pain at seeing our Lord's suffering that I couldn't have helped crying and shouting out, even if it had cost me my life. And this was the first outcry I ever made during any vision.

And this sort of crying out persisted for many years afterwards. No one could stop it, and I was severely condemned and criticized for it. So loud and so remarkable was it, people were astounded unless they had heard it before or knew the cause of the yelling. And I had these attacks so often that they sapped my bodily strength, especially if I heard about our Lord's passion. And sometimes when I saw the crucifix, or if I saw a man or any animal with an open wound, or if a man beat a child in front of me, or if I saw or heard someone striking a horse or another beast with a whip, I imagined that I was witnessing our Lord being beaten or wounded just like the man or the beast; and this was the case as much in the country as in the town, and when I was by myself as well as with other people.

When my crying fits began I had them frequently. This was the case in Jerusalem and also in Rome. But when I first came home to England they occurred only seldom—say once a month—but then once a week, and afterwards daily. Once I had fourteen in a day, on another day seven—all according to God's visitations. Sometimes when God sent them I was in the church; at other times I was in the street, or indoors, or in the countryside, for I never knew the time or hour when they would come. And they never came without overwhelmingly sweet devotion and intense inner vision.

And as soon as I realized that I was going to cry out, I contained it for as long as I could, so that people would not be disturbed by the noise. For some said I was troubled by an evil spirit; some said it was an illness and some said I had drunk too much wine; some cursed me and wanted me in an asylum; some wished that I was out at sea in a bottomless boat: everyone had his own idea. Other, spiritually-minded people loved me and favoured me all the more. Some great scholars said that neither our Lady nor any of the Saints in heaven had ever cried so much, but they had very little idea what I felt; nor would they accept that I couldn't stop myself crying out, even if I had wanted to. So, when I knew that I was about to cry out, I kept it in for as long as I could and did my best to hold it back. I suppressed it until I had turned a greyish blue like lead, but it kept growing bigger and bigger inside me, ready for the time when it would escape. And when my body could no longer stand the inner ferment, when it was overcome with the inexpressible love that worked so fervently in my soul, then I fell down and cried out wondrously loud. And the more I tried to keep it in or hold it at bay the longer and louder I cried in the end. That is what I did on the mount of Calvary, as I have already said.

I witnessed things so vividly with my inner vision that it seemed as if Christ was hanging before my eyes in his manhood. And when, by the outpouring of the high mercy of our Sovereign Saviour Jesus Christ, I was allowed to see so palpably his precious tender body, ripped and torn by scourges, with more gashes than the holes in a dovecote, hanging on the cross and bearing the crown of thorns on his head, his blessed hands and his tender feet nailed to the hard wood, the rivers of blood profusely flowing from every part, the grave and dreadful wound in his precious side shedding blood and water out of love for me and for my salvation, then I fell to the ground and cried aloud, twisting and turning amazingly in every direction, flinging out my arms as if I was in my death throes. And nothing could keep me from crying out or from making these bodily movements, such was the fire of love that burned so ardently in my soul with pure pity and compassion.

At the end of her book, Margery prays

"As for my wailing and sobbing and weeping, Lord God Almighty, you know what scorn, humiliation, contempt and blame they have brought upon me; and you know that it isn't within my own power to weep aloud or silently, no matter what feelings of devotion or sweetness come upon me, since all my tears are a blessing from the Holy Spirit. This being so, Lord, excuse me in the eyes of the world and help people to realize and understand that you do this work and bestow this gift to glorify your name and to make their love for you greater. And, sovereign Lord Christ Jesus, may my crying and weeping save as many people as have scorned me for it, or shall do until the end of the world— many more if that is your will.

"So far as earthly love is concerned, all I want is to love God supremely and to love other creatures for him and in him. This being so, I ask you to quench all carnal desire both in me and in all whose human form has shown me the shape of your own blessed body.

"Lord, suffuse our hearts with a holy fear of you, for the sake of your cruel wounds. Make my confessors fear you in me and love you in me, and by virtue of the grief that you've given me for the sins of others make everyone grieve all the more for their own sins. Good Jesus, make my will yours and your will mine so that I shall have no will but yours alone."

. . . .

"Lord Christ Jesus, I thank you for all health and all wealth, for all riches and all poverty, for sickness, scorn, spite, injustice, and all the various troubles which have befallen me or shall do so for as long as I live; and I give you great thanks for any pain you allow me to suffer in this earthly life to atone for my sins and increase my store of merit in heaven. Lord, hear my prayers, for I sincerely have every reason to thank you."

. . . .

"My soul praises God and all of you who dwell in heaven. May God be blessed in all of you and may you all be blessed in God. Lord, may you be honoured for all your mercies to those in heaven and those on earth. Lord, I especially give you thanks for Mary Magdalene, Mary of Egypt, St Paul and St Augustine. As you showed them your mercy, so show it to me and to all who appeal to your merciful heart.

"May I inherit the peace and repose you left your disciples and those who loved you, and may I enjoy it on earth and in heaven for evermore."

. . . .

"Thank you, Lord, for all the sins you have kept me from committing and thank you, Lord, for all the troubles you have made me suffer for those which I have committed. For these and all the other mercies which are necessary for me and for every living creature on earth, I thank you, Lord.

"As for all those who put their faith and trust in my prayers, or shall do so until the end of the world, I ask you, Lord, to grant them, of your abundant mercy, such blessings in spirit or body as they may desire for the good of their souls. Amen."

George Herbert

The medlar tree in the garden
of Bemerton Rectory (see pp. 139-40)

GEORGE HERBERT

In the century and a half between the death of Margery Kempe around 1440 and the birth of George Herbert in 1593, winds of profound change blew across Europe, reshaping the contours of medieval life into the emerging structures of the modern age. With the Renaissance, the spirit of individualism and intellectual exploration swept from Italy across the Continent and the Channel and stimulated a wave of humanistic endeavours in many fields. The Protestant Reformation shook the foundations of Church authority and inspired personal religious responsibility and individual encounters with the Word of God in Scripture. Shakespeare's *Hamlet* and *The Tempest* made their first entrance on the stage of Western culture and imagination during Herbert's formative years in the early seventeenth century. And the spirit of modern science was slowly transforming the idea of nature and the human sense of connection to it, with Bacon's *Advancement of Learning* appearing in 1605 and Galileo's trial and condemnation occurring in 1633, the year of Herbert's death.

Herbert was born in the shadow of Montgomery Castle, which had been owned by his family for many years, just across the Welsh border from Shropshire.[1] It is rather surprising that a man of such great literary talents and spiritual sensitivity should have emerged from a family so firmly established in the British aristocracy and known more for military and political prowess than for religious pursuits. The nurturing of Herbert's unusually rich inner life seems to have occurred in large measure through the stimulating influence of his mother, Magdalen, a woman of intelligence and literary tastes and a close friend and patron of John Donne, whose work had a formative effect not only on George Herbert but on the other English metaphysical poets as well.

Lady Herbert, whose husband died when George was three, moved the family to Oxford in 1599 and, more permanently, to London in 1601. At Westminster School Herbert not only mastered the fundamentals of the grammar school, but also developed musical abilities, an interest and sensitivity echoed in the content of some of his poems and in the lyrical style of many others. He entered Trinity College, Cambridge, in 1609, and was soon to become one of its most brilliant young stars. In 1610 he sent his mother a New Year's gift in the form of a letter consisting of two sonnets and a pledge, saying that "for my own part, my meaning (dear Mother) is in these Sonnets, to declare my resolution to be, that my poor Abilities in Poetry, shall be all, and ever consecrated to Gods glory."[2]

It was a number of years, however, before Herbert turned his entire life explicitly toward such a purpose. He first held several academic posts at Cambridge, obtaining the coveted position of Public Orator in 1620, and was elected member of Parliament for Montgomery borough in 1624. In these influential public offices, Herbert broadened his acquaintance with some of the leading political and religious figures of the day, most notably Sir Francis Bacon, Lord Chancellor of England, and Bishop Lancelot Andrewes. But in the wake of Bacon's fall from power, and following the deaths of two probable patrons (and soon that of King James I), Herbert's worldly ambitions diminished and in 1624 he followed the aspirations of his poetry with the direction of his life. He was ordained a deacon and in 1626 became canon of Lincoln Cathedral and prebendary for the church of Leighton Bromswold in Huntingdonshire. Then, in 1630, two years after resigning as orator at Cambridge and one year after marrying Jane Danvers, Herbert was ordained a priest and became rector of the parish of Bemerton, near Salisbury. Here he served with great devotion until he succumbed to tuberculosis on 1 March 1633.

Herbert's celebrated (though not fully reliable) biographer, Izaak Walton, recorded that as Herbert became aware of his impending death, he sent to his friend Nicholas Ferrar at Little Gidding the collection of poems he had been writing over the previous few years and that is now known as *The Temple*. He informed Ferrar that it contains "a picture of the many spiritual conflicts that have past betwixt God and my soul," and he asked his friend to have it published if he thought it "may turn to the advantage of any dejected poor soul," but if not, to burn it.[3] *The Temple* was first published in the year of Herbert's death and over the centuries has continued to attract a great deal of both popular and scholarly attention, establishing him as one of the leading English poets of his time.

A distinctive feature of *The Temple* is its depiction of struggle and searching. In both the structure of individual poems and the pattern of the whole collection, Herbert presents a story of the gradual progress or ascent of the soul to God. He seems to be offering not only a description of his own or another's experience, but also an invitation to his readers to participate in this process themselves, to tread sympathetically this pilgrim's often uncertain path.

The Temple is rich with evocative imagery, some of the most pervasive and significant being the allusions to the natural world. For Herbert, the objects and events of nature were seen, at least potentially, as aspects of God's communication with humankind. The "fair oak, or bush, or cave," the cycle of the seasons, are all elements—"visible words"—in a divine language through which God's presence and purpose are disclosed. The meaning of these signs, however, is often far from clear. Herbert believed that humankind, ever since the Fall, has been afflicted with a kind of "illiteracy" with regard to reading divine intimations, not only in the Book of Nature, but also in the Book of Scripture. The spiritual journey we are invited to follow in *The Temple* involves the gradual process of learning to interpret divine signs, of cultivating a form of spiritual literacy that will enable us to see beyond the fragmented and superficial appearances of things to the inner and unified message of the whole. As Herbert expresses it in "The Flower," "Thy word is all, if we could spell." And as he is intent on showing throughout *The Temple*, a central theme of the message imprinted in both divine Books is the unfailing providence and affection of the Author for the reader.[4]

Herbert's method of making sense of the Book of Nature is

based on the idea that the divine Spirit—the Word—that in-
forms the Book of Scripture also orders and enlivens the Book of
Nature and inspires the human mind and heart. All of these
interpenetrating manifestations of the Word are taken as aspects
of the Incarnation, in which the Spirit transforms and divinizes
the flesh and matter of the world. A recent writer has noted that
"reading Herbert's poems is like—indeed is—overhearing a conversation between a faithful Christian soul and God. . . . We have
only Herbert's words, but, if we listen, we can hear in the silence
surrounding them the replies of God."[5] Herbert's writings are of a
piece with his life, not merely descriptions of the ongoing Incarnation, but, as our reading of them perhaps also can be, occasions
for the activity of the Word.

It is important, considering the course on which Western culture was about to embark in the early seventeenth century, to
notice that Herbert's reading of the Book of Nature was somewhat different from that proposed by natural philosophers such as
Bacon and Galileo. Although Herbert admired his friend Bacon
for his various achievements, the two men were of quite different
tenors of mind. Bacon's way of reading the Book of Nature was
motivated, as was Galileo's assertion that this Book is written in
the language of mathematics, by the demands of science for the
measurement and manipulation of nature. Herbert's method, on
the other hand, was generated primarily by the desire for a fuller
measure of divine converse. For him, nature, properly perceived,
could become the occasion of a unifying epiphany; for the emerging modern scientists, nature, though containing evidence of
divine design, was likely to be the occasion for analysis and for
translation of the language of nature into the practical purposes of
the world.

Herbert's other major book, entitled *A Priest to the Temple*, but
commonly known by its subtitle, *The Country Parson*, reflects his
life as a parish priest at Bemerton from 1630 to 1633. In this
prose work Herbert painted his picture of the model pastor,
saying in a note to the reader that "I will set [my mark] as high as
I can, since he shoots higher that threatens the Moon, than he
that aims at a tree." *The Country Parson* contains collected pieces

of wisdom and advice, and displays the common sense of one with wide experience and insight into both the possibilities and the failings of human nature. It shows Herbert, or any good priest in innumerable country parishes, participating in the lives of his parishioners, who included members of various social classes and stations in life, as he attempts to facilitate their dealings with each other and their dedication to God.

The centre of Herbert's activities in Bemerton (though he was also responsible for the parish church of Fugglestone St Peter) was the chapel of St Andrew. In this building, which dates from the fourteenth century, Herbert was inducted into the priesthood on 26 April 1630 and then faithfully performed his daily pastoral services, including Matins at ten and Evensong at four, as well as catechizing, preaching, and teaching. Herbert is also buried here, and although the exact location of his grave is not known, it is either beneath or to the north of the altar.

Across the road from St Andrew's is the Bemerton Rectory, where Herbert lived. This dwelling was somewhat more humble than the several Herbert had known earlier, the household here including, in addition to the parson and his wife, three of their orphaned nieces, four maidservants, and two menservants. The rectory has been expanded from its seventeenth-century dimensions, additions having been built on the east, west, and north sides, but the original outlines are still evident in the heavy beams and the great fireplace.

From the southern side of the rectory the Book of Nature opened up pleasingly, and from Herbert's bedroom he could look out on a garden and a lawn sloping down to the River Nadder and the watery meadows beyond. The story of struggle and divine sustenance, and the cycle of death and regeneration, which Herbert often portrayed in his poetry, is evident in the inhabitants of this garden. A fig tree which is said to have survived from Herbert's time is still a resident here. A medlar apparently died around the turn of the century, but in 1906 a small shoot appeared. At this sign of hope, Kew Gardens planted a whitethorn next to it and in 1908 the two plants were joined. The tree vigorously pursued its tortuous destiny until its roots were attacked by honey fungus in 1973. To provide a further form of sustenance, quince grafts have been attempted since that time.

At the river's edge, one can see the towering spire of Salisbury Cathedral. Herbert typically walked the mile from Bemerton to Salisbury twice a week, where he enjoyed what he considered one of the most sublime of earthly delights—the music of the cathedral. He would attend Evensong at Salisbury and, afterward, would participate in private "musick-meetings," in which he played the lute and perhaps sang. It is even possible that Herbert sang some of his own poems here and accompanied himself on his lute. Some of the interesting encounters he made on his walks to Salisbury, to experience the sense of "heaven upon earth" engendered by the music, were recorded by Walton and are included in the selections that follow.

The splendid early English Gothic architecture of Salisbury Cathedral would certainly have assisted the transport Herbert felt within its walls, with its colourful columns and ribbed vault, and its spire reaching heavenward some 404 feet, the highest in England. The cathedral was built mainly between 1220 and 1260, some of the materials coming from the great cathedral at Old Sarum, which was torn down when the bishopric was moved to New Sarum (Salisbury) in 1220. The cloister and octagonal chapter house attached to the cathedral give the impression of a monastery, although Salisbury has never housed monks and has always been administered by a brotherhood of canons under the presidency of its dean.

Notes

1. This account is based largely on Amy M. Charles, *A Life of George Herbert* (Ithaca, NY: Cornell University Press, 1977). The extracts from *The Temple* and *The Country Parson* that follow are taken from *The Complete Works in Verse and Prose of George Herbert*, edited by Rev. Alexander B. Grosart, (an edition of 100 copies only, printed privately in 1874; reprinted New York: AMS Press, 1982.) The same texts are also available in an edition of 1941 (note 2 below); *The Temple* and *The Country Parson* are also published in the U.S. by the Paulist Press (1981). The spelling, and occasional wording, have here been slightly modernized.

2. *The Works of George Herbert*, edited by F. E. Hutchinson (Oxford: Clarendon Press, 1941), p. 363.

3. Izaak Walton, *The Life of Mr. George Herbert* (London: Marriott, 1670; reprinted in *The Complete Works in Verse and Prose of George Herbert*, p. 73. The final extract is taken from this work.

4. See Richard Todd, *The Opacity of Signs: Acts of Interpretation in George Herbert's "The Temple"* (Columbia, Mo.: University of Missouri Press, 1986) for an in-depth discussion.

5. Lucy Beckett, "Heaven in the Ordinary," *The Tablet* (25 September 1993), p. 1228.

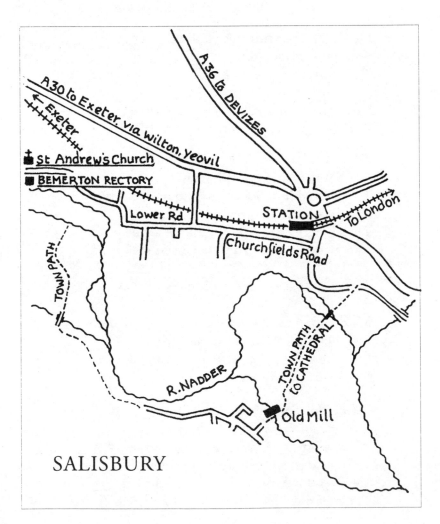

16. *AFFLICTION*

When first thou didst entice to thee my heart,
    I thought the service brave:
So many joys I writ down for my part,
    Besides what I might have
Out of my stock of natural delights,
Augmented with thy grace's perquisites.

I lookèd on thy furniture so fine
    And made it fine to me;
Thy glorious household-stuff did me entwine,
    And 'tice me unto thee;
Such stars I counted mine: both heav'n and earth
Paid me my wages in a world of mirth.

What pleasures could I want, whose King I served,
    Where joys my fellows were?
Thus argu'd into hopes, my thoughts reserved
    No place for grief or fear;
Therefore my sudden soul caught at the place,
And made her youth and fierceness seek thy face.

At first thou gav'st me milk and sweetness,
    I had my wish and way;
My days were straw'd with flowers and happ'nesses;
    There was no month but May.
But with my years sorrow did twist and grow,
And made a party unawares for woe.

My flesh begun into my soul in pain,
    Sicknesses cleave my bones,
Consuming agues dwell in ev'ry vein,
    And tune my breath to groans:
Sorrow was all my soul; I scarce believed,
Till grief did tell me roundly, that I lived.

When I got health, thou took'st away my life,
  And more—for my friends die:
My mirth and edge was lost, a blunted knife
  Was of more use than I:
Thus thin and lean, without a fence or friend,
I was blown through with ev'ry storm and wind.

Whereas my birth and spirit rather took
  The way that takes the town,
Thou didst betray me to a ling'ring book,
  And wrap me in a gown;
I was entangled in the world of strife
Before I had the power to change my life.

Yet, for I threatened oft the siege to raise,
  Not simp'ring all mine age,
Thou often did with academic praise
  Melt and dissolve my rage:
I took thy sweetened pill till I came near;
I could not go away, nor persevere.

Yet lest perchance I should too happy be
  In my unhappiness,
Turning my purge to food, thou throwest me
  Into more sicknesses:
Thus doth thy power cross-bias me, not making
Thine own gift good, yet me from my ways taking.

Now I am here, what wilt thou do with me
  None of my books will show:
I read, and sigh, and wish I were a tree—
  For sure then I should grow
To fruit or shade; at least some bird would trust
Her household to me, and I should be just.

Yet, though thou troublest me, I must be meek;
  In weakness must be stout.

Well, I will change the service, and go seek
    Some other master out.
Ah, my dear God, though I am clean forgot,
Let me not love thee, if I love thee not.

17. REPENTANCE

    Lord, I confess my sin is great;
    Great is my sin: O gently treat
With thy quick flow'r thy momentary bloom,
      Whose life still pressing
      Is one undressing,
A steady aiming at a tomb.

    Man's age is two hours' work, or three;
    Each day doth round about us see.
Thus are we to delights, but we are all
      To sorrows old,
      If life be told
From what life feeleth, Adam's fall.

    O let thy height of mercy, then,
    Compassionate short-breathèd men;
Cut me not off for my most foul transgression:
      I do confess
      My foolishness;
My God, accept of my confession.

    Sweeten at length this bitter bowl
    Which thou hast pour'd into my soul;
Thy wormwood turn to health, winds to fair weather:
      For if thou stay,
      I and this day,
As we did rise, we die together.

    When thou for sin rebukest man,
    Forthwith he waxeth woe and wan;

Bitterness fills our bowels, all our hearts
      Pine and decay
      And drop away,
   And carry with them th'other parts.

   But thou wilt sin and grief destroy;
   That so the broken bones may joy,
And tune together in a well-set song,
      Full of his praises
      Who dead men raises.
   Fractures well cur'd make us more strong.

90. *PROVIDENCE*

O sacred Providence, who from end to end
Strongly and sweetly movest! shall I write,
And not of thee, through whom my fingers bend
To hold my quill? shall they not do thee right?

Of all the creatures both in sea and land,
Only to man thou hast made known thy ways,
And put the pen alone into his hand,
And made him secretary of thy praise.

Beasts fain would sing; birds ditty to their notes;
Trees would be tuning on their native lute
To thy renown: but all their hands and throats
Are brought to man, while they are lame and mute.

Man is the world's high-priest: he doth present
The sacrifice for all; while they below
Unto the service mutter an assent,
Such as springs use that fall, and winds that blow.

He that to praise and laud thee doth refrain,
Doth not refrain unto himself alone,
But robs a thousand who would praise thee fain,
And doth commit a world of sins in one.

145

The beasts say, "Eat me"; but if beasts must teach,
The tongue is yours to eat, but mine to praise:
The trees say, "Pull me"; but the hand you stretch
Is mine to write, as it is yours to raise.

Wherefore, most sacred Spirit, I here present,
For me and all my fellows, praise to thee;
And just it is that I should pay the rent,
Because the benefit accrues to me.

We all acknowledge both thy power and love
To be exact, transcendent, and divine;
Who dost so strongly and so sweetly move,
While all things have their will, yet none but thine.

For either thy command or thy permission
Lay hands on all; they are thy right and left;
The first puts on with speed and expedition;
The other curbs sin's stealing pace and theft.

Nothing escapes them both; all must appear,
And be disposed, and dressed, and tuned by thee,
Who sweetly temper'st all. If we could hear
Thy skill and art, what music would it be!

Thou art in small things great, not small in any;
Thy even praise can neither rise nor fall;
Thou art in all things one, in each thing many;
For thou art infinite in one and all.

Tempests are calm to thee; they know thy hand,
And hold it fast, as children do their father's,
Which cry and follow: thou hast made poor sand
Check the proud sea, ev'n when it swells and gathers.

Thy cupboard serves the world: the meat is set
Where all may reach; no beast but knows his feed:

Birds teach us hawking; fishes have their net;
The great prey on the less, they on some weed.

Nothing engender'd doth prevent* his meat;
Flies have their table spread ere they appear;
Some creatures have in winter what to eat;
Others to sleep, and envy not their cheer.

How finely dost thou times and seasons spin,
And make a twist checkered with night and day,
Which, as it lengthens, winds and winds us in,
As bowls go on, but turning all the way!

Each creature hath a wisdom for his good;
The pigeons feed their tender offspring, crying
When they are callow, but withdraw their food
When they are fledged, that need may teach them flying.

Bees work for man; and yet they never bruise
Their master's flower; but leave it, having done,
As fair as ever and as fit to use;
So both the flower doth stay and honey run.

Sheep eat the grass, and dung the ground for more;
Trees after bearing drop their leaves for soil;
Springs vent their streams, and by expense, get store;
Clouds cool by heat, and baths by cooling boil.

Who hath the virtue to express the rare
And curious virtues both of herbs and stones?
Is there a herb for that? O that thy care
Would show a root that gives expressions!

And if an herb hath power, what have the stars?
A rose, besides its beauty, is a cure:

---

*The meaning is "come before" (ed.).

Doubtless our plagues and plenty, peace and wars,
Are there much surer than our art is sure.

Thou hast hid metals: man may take them thence,
But at his peril; when he digs the place
He makes a grave; as if the thing had sense,
And threaten'd man that he should fill the space.

Ev'n poisons praise thee: should a thing be lost?
Should creatures want, for want of heed, their due?
Since where are poisons, antidotes are most;
The help stands close, and keeps the fear in view.

The sea, which seems to stop the traveller,
Is by a ship the speedier passage made;
The winds, who think they rule the mariner,
Are ruled by him, and taught to serve his trade.

And as thy house is full, so I adore
Thy curious art in marshalling thy goods.
The hills with wealth abound, the vales with store;
The South with marble; North with furs and woods.

Hard things are glorious, easy things good cheap;
The common all men have; that which is rare
Men therefore seek to have, and care to keep.
The healthy frosts with summer fruits compare.

Light without wind is glass; warm without weight
Is wool and furs; cool without closeness, shade;
Speed without pains, a horse; tall without height,
A servile hawk; low without loss, a spade.

All countries have enough to serve their need:
If they seek fine things, thou dost make them run
For their offence, and then dost turn their speed
To be commerce and trade from sun to sun.

George Herbert

Nothing wears clothes but man; nothing doth need
But he to wear them; nothing useth fire
But man alone, to show his heav'nly breed;
And only he hath fuel in desire.

When th'earth was dry, thou mad'st a sea of wet;
When that lay gathered, thou didst broach the mountains;
When yet some place could no moisture get,
The winds grew gard'ners, and the clouds good fountains.

Rain, do not hurt my flowers, but gently spend
Your honey-drops: press not to smell them here;
When they are ripe, their odour will ascend,
And at your lodging with their thanks appear.

How harsh are thorns to pears! and yet they make
A better hedge, and need less reparation.
How smooth are silks comparèd with a stake
Or with a stone! yet make no good foundation.

Sometimes thou dost divide thy gifts to man,
Sometimes unite; the Indian nut* alone
Is clothing, meat and trencher, drink and can,
Boat, cable, sail, and needle, all in one.

Most herbs that grow in brooks are hot and dry,
Cold fruits' warm kernels help against the wind;
The lemon's juice and rind cure mutually;
The whey of milk doth loose, the milk doth bind.

Thy creatures leap not, but express a feast,
Where all the guests sit close, and nothing wants:
Frogs marry fish and flesh; bats, bird and beast;
Sponges, non-sense and sense; mines, th'earth and plants.

*I.e., the coconut (ed.)

149

To show thou art not bound, as if thy lot
Were worse than ours, sometimes thou shiftest hands:
Most things move th'under-jaw, the crocodile not;
Most things sleep lying, th'elephant leans or stands.

But who hath praise enough? nay, who hath any?
None can express thy works but he that knows them
And none can know thy works, which are so many
And so complete, but only he that owns them.

All things that are, though they have sev'ral ways,
Yet in their being join with one advice
To honour thee; and so I give thee praise
In all my other hymns, but in this twice.

Each thing that is, although in use and name
It go for one, hath many ways in store
To honour thee; and so each hymn the fame
Extolleth many ways, yet this one more.

132. *The Flower*

How fresh, O lord, how sweet and clean
Are thy returns! ev'n as the flowers in Spring,
    To which, besides their own demean,
The late-past frosts tributes of pleasures bring;
            Grief melts away
            Like snow in May,
    As if there were no such cold thing.

Who would have thought my shrivelled heart
Could have recovered greenness? It was gone
    Quite under ground; as flowers depart
To see their mother-root, when they have blown,
            Where they together
            All the hard weather,
    Dead to the world, keep house unknown.

150

These are thy wonders, Lord of power.
Killing and quick'ning, bringing down to hell
    And up to heaven in an hour;
Making a chiming of a passing-bell.
        We say amiss
        This or that is;
    Thy word is all, if we could spell.

    O that I once past changing were,
Fast in thy paradise, where no flower can wither!
    Many a Spring I shoot up fair,
Off'ring at heav'n, growing and groaning thither;
        Nor doth my flower
        Want a Spring shower,
    My sins and I joining together.

    But while I grow in a straight line,
Still upwards bent, as if heav'n were mine own
    Thy anger comes, and I decline:
What frost to that? what pole is not the zone
        Where all things burn,
        When thou dost turn,
    And the least frown of thine is shown?

    And now in age I bud again,
After so many deaths I live and write;
    I once more smell the dew and rain,
And relish versing: O, my only light,
        It cannot be
        That I am he
    On whom thy tempests fell all night.

    These are thy wonders, Lord of love,
To make us see we are but flowers that glide;
    Which when we once can find and prove,
Thou hast a garden for us where to bide.
        Who would be more,
        Swelling through store,
    Forfeit their paradise by their pride.

THE COUNTRY PARSON

CHAPTER 1. *OF A PASTOR*

A pastor is the deputy of Christ for the reducing of man to the obedience of God. This definition is evident, and contains the direct steps of pastoral duty and authority. For, first man fell from God by disobedience. Second, Christ is the glorious instrument of God for the revoking of man. Third, Christ being not to continue on earth, but after he had fulfilled the work of reconciliation to be received up into heaven, he constituted deputies in his place; and these are priests. And therefore St Paul, in the beginning of his Epistles, professes this, and in [that] to the Colossians, plainly affirms that "in my flesh I am completing what is lacking in Christ's afflictions for the sake of his body, that is, the church."* Wherein is contained the complete definition of a minister. Out of this charter of the priesthood may be plainly gathered both the dignity thereof and the duty: the dignity, in that a priest may do that which Christ did, and by his authority and as his vice-regent; the duty, in that a priest is to do what Christ did, and after his manner, both for doctrine and life.

CHAPTER 3. *THE PARSON'S LIFE*

The country parson is exceeding exact in his life, being holy, just, prudent, temperate, bold, grave, in all his ways. And because the two highest points of life wherein a Christian is most seen are patience and mortification—patience in regard of afflictions; mortification in regard of lusts and affections, and the stupefying and deadening of all the clamorous powers of the soul—therefore he has thoroughly studied these, that he may be an absolute master and commander of himself for all the purposes [for] which God has ordained him.

Yet in these points he labours most in those things which are most apt to scandalize his parish. And first, because country people live hardly, and therefore as feeling their own sweat, and

---

*Col. 1:24. NRSV used here (ed.)

consequently knowing the price of money, are offended much with any who by hard usage increase their travail, the country parson is very circumspect in avoiding all covetousness, neither being greedy to get, nor niggardly to keep, nor troubled to lose any worldly wealth; but in all his words and actions slighting and disesteeming it, even to a wondering that the world should so much value wealth, which in the day of wrath has not one dram of comfort for us.

Second, because luxury is a very visible sin, the parson is very careful to avoid all the kinds thereof; but especially that of drinking, because it is the most popular vice, into which, if he come, he prostitutes himself both to shame and sin, and, by having fellowship with "the unfruitful works of darkness" (Eph. 5:11), he disables himself of authority to reprove them; for sins make all equal whom they find together, and then they are worst who ought to be best. Neither is it for the servant of God to haunt inns or taverns or alehouses, to the dishonour of his person and office. The parson does not so, but orders his life in such a fashion, that when death takes him, as the Jews and Judas did Christ, he may say as Christ did, "I sat daily with you teaching in the Temple" (Matt. 26:55).

Third, because country people (as indeed all honest men) do much esteem their word, it being the life of buying and selling and dealing in the world, therefore the parson is very strict in keeping his word, though it be to his own hindrance, as knowing that if he be not so he will quickly be discovered and disregarded: neither will they believe him in the pulpit whom they cannot trust in his conversation. As for oaths and apparel, the disorders thereof are also very manifest. The parson's yea is yea, and nay nay; and his apparel plain, but reverend and clean, without spots or dust or smell; the purity of his mind breaking out and dilating itself even to his body, clothes and habitation.

CHAPTER 4. *THE PARSON'S KNOWLEDGE*

The country parson is full of all knowledge. They say that it is an ill mason that refuses any stone; and there is no knowledge but, in a skilful hand, serves either positively as it is, or else to illustrate some other knowledge. He condescends even to the knowledge of tillage and pastorage, and makes great use of them in teaching, because people, by what they understand, are best led to what they understand not. But the chief and top of his knowledge consists in the book of books, the storehouse and magazine of life and comfort, the Holy Scriptures. There he sucks and lives.

In the Scriptures he finds four things: precepts for life, doctrines for knowledge, examples for illustration, and promises for comfort. These he has digested severally. But for the understanding of these, the means he uses are first, a holy life, remembering what his Master says, that "anyone who resolves to do the will of God will know whether the teaching is from God" (John 7:17); and assuring himself that wicked men, however learned, do not know the Scriptures, because they feel them not, and because they are not understood but with the same Spirit that wrote them.

The second means is prayer, which if it be necessary even in temporal things, how much more in things of another world, where the well is deep, and we have nothing of ourselves to draw with? Wherefore he ever begins the reading of the Scripture with some short inward ejaculation, as "Lord, open my eyes, so that I may behold wondrous things out of thy law" (Ps. 119:18).

The third means is a diligent collation of Scripture with Scripture. For all truth being consonant to itself, and all being penned by one and the self-same Spirit, it cannot be but an industrious and judicious comparing of place with place must be a singular help for the right understanding of the Scriptures. To this may be added the consideration of any text with the coherence thereof, touching what goes before and what follows after, as also the scope of the Holy Ghost. When the Apostles would have called down fire from heaven, they were reproved, as ignorant of what spirit they were. For the law required one thing, and the gospel another; yet as diverse, not as repugnant; therefore the spirit of both is to be considered and weighed.

The fourth means are commentators and Fathers who have handled the places controverted, which the parson by no means refuses. As he does not so study others as to neglect the grace of

154

God in himself, and what the Holy Spirit teaches him, so does he assure himself that God in all ages has had his servants, to whom he has revealed his truth as well as to him; and that as one country does not bear all things, that there may be a commerce, so neither has God opened, or will open, all to one, that there may be a traffic in knowledge between the servants of God, for the planting both of love and humility. Wherefore he has one commentary at least upon every book of Scripture; and ploughing with this and his own meditations, he enters into the secrets of God treasured in the Holy Scripture.

Chapter 30. *The Parson's Consideration of Providence*

The country parson, considering the great aptitude country people have to think that all things come by a kind of natural course, and that if they sow and [manure] their grounds they must have corn, if they keep and fodder well their cattle they must have milk and calves, labours well to reduce them to see God's hand in all things, and to believe that things are not set in such an inevitable order, but that God often changes it according as he sees fit, either for reward or punishment.

To this end he represents to his flock that God has and exercises a threefold power in every thing which concerns man. The first is a sustaining power, the second is a governing power, the third a spiritual power. By his sustaining power he preserves and actuates every thing in its being, so that corn does not grow by any other virtue than by that which he continually supplies, as the corn needs it; without which supply the corn would instantly dry up, as a river would if the fountain were stopped. And it is observable that if any thing could presume of an inevitable course and constancy in its operations, certainly it should be either the sun in heaven or the fire on earth, by reason of their fierce, strong and violent natures; yet when God pleased, the sun stood still, the fire burned not.

By God's governing power he preserves and orders the references of things one to the other, so that though the corn do grow and be preserved in that act by his sustaining power, yet if he suit not other things to the growth, as seasons and weather, and other accidents, by his governing power, the fairest harvests come to nothing. And it is observable that God delights to have men feel and acknowledge and reverence his power, and therefore he often overturns things when they are thought past danger; that is his time of interposing: as when a merchant has a ship come home after many a storm which it has escaped, he destroys it sometimes in the very haven; or if the goods be housed, a fire has broken forth and suddenly consumed them.

Now this he does that men should perpetuate and not break off their acts of dependence, how fair soever the opportunities present themselves. So that if a farmer should depend upon God all the year, and being ready to put hand to sickle shall then secure himself, and think all cocksure, then God sends such weather as lays the corn and destroys it; or if he depend on God further, even till he [gather his corn into the barn], and then think all sure, God sends a fire and consumes all that he has; for that he ought not to break off, but to continue his dependence upon God, not only before the corn is [gathered in], but after also, and indeed to depend and fear continually.

The third power is spiritual, by which God turns all outward blessings to inward advantages. So that if a farmer has both a fair harvest, and that also well [gathered in] and continuing safe there, yet if God give him not the grace to use and utter this well, all his advantages are to his loss. Better were his corn burnt than not spiritually improved. And it is observable in this how God's goodness strives with man's refractoriness: man would sit down at this world; God bids him sell it and purchase a better. Just as a father who has in his hand an apple and a piece of gold under it: the child comes, and with pulling gets the apple out of his father's hand; his father bids him throw it away, and he will give him the gold for it; which the child utterly refusing, eats [the apple] and is troubled with worms. So is the carnal and wilful man, with the worm of the grave in this world and the worm of conscience in the next.

George Herbert

PRAYER AFTER SERMON

Blessed be God and the Father of all mercy, who continues to pour his benefits upon us. Thou hast elected us, thou hast called us, thou hast justified us, sanctified and glorified us; thou wast born for us, and thou livedst and diedst for us; thou hast given us the blessings of this life and of a better. O Lord, thy blessings hang in clusters, they come trooping upon us, they break forth like mighty waters on every side. And now, Lord, thou hast fed us with the bread of life; so man did eat angels' food. O Lord, bless it, make it health and strength unto us; still striving and prospering so long within us, until our obedience reach thy measure of thy love, who hast done for us as much as may be. Grant this, dear Father, for thy Son's sake, our only Saviour, to whom with thee and the Holy Ghost, three persons but one most glorious incomprehensible God, be ascribed all honour, and glory, and praise, ever. Amen.

THE LIFE OF Mr GEORGE HERBERT
by Isaak Walton

As his desire to enjoy his heaven upon earth* drew him twice every week to Salisbury, so his walks thither were the occasion of many happy accidents to others, of which I will mention some few.

In one of his walks to Salisbury he overtook a gentleman that is still living in that city; and in their walk together Mr Herbert took a fair occasion to talk with him, and humbly begged to be excused if he asked him some account of his faith, and said, "I do this the rather because, though you are not of my parish, yet I receive tithe from you by the hand of your tenant; and, sir, I am the bolder to do it, because I know there to be some sermon-hearers that be like those fishes that always live in salt water, and yet are always fresh." After which expression Mr Herbert asked him some needful questions; and having received his answer, gave him such rules for the trial of his sincerity and for a practical piety, and in so loving and meek a manner, that the gentleman did so fall in love with him and his discourse, that he would often contrive to meet him in his walk to Salisbury, or to attend him back to Bemerton, and still mentions the name of Mr George Herbert with veneration, and still praises God that he knew him.

In another of his Salisbury walks he met with a neighbour minister; and after some friendly discourse betwixt them, and some condolement for the wickedness of the times and contempt of the clergy, Mr Herbert took occasion to say, "One cure for these distempers would be for the clergy to keep the Ember-weeks strictly, and beg of their parishioners to join with them in fasting and prayers for a more religious clergy." And another cure would be "for them to restore the great and neglected duty of catechizing, on which the salvation of so many of the poor and ignorant lay people does depend; but principally that the clergy themselves would be sure to live unblameably, and that the dignified clergy especially, who preach temperance, would avoid surfeiting, and

---

*In the music group in which he played and sang in Salisbury (ed.)

take all occasions to express a visible humility and charity in their lives; for this would force a love and an imitation and an unfeigned reverence from all that knew them. . . . "This," said Mr Herbert, "would be a cure for the wickedness and growing atheism of our age. And, my dear brother, till this is done by us, and done in earnest, let no man expect a reformation of the manners of the laity; for 'tis not learning, but this, this only, that must do it; and till then the fault must lie at our doors."

In another walk to Salisbury he saw a poor man, with a poorer horse, that was fallen under its load. They were both in distress, and needed present help; which Mr Herbert perceiving, put off his canonical coat, and helped the poor man to unload, and after to load his horse. The poor man blessed him for it and he blessed the poor man, and was so like the good Samaritan that he gave him money to refresh both himself and his horse, and told him that if he loved himself, he should be merciful to his beast. Thus he left the poor man; and at his coming to his musical friends at Salisbury, they began to wonder that Mr George Herbert, who used to be so trim and clean, came into that company so soiled and discomposed; but he told them the occasion; and when one of the company told him he had disparaged himself by so dirty an employment, his answer was, that the thought of what he had done would prove music to him at midnight, and the omission of it would have upbraided and made discord in his conscience whensoever he should pass by that place, "For if I be bound to pray for all that be in distress, I am sure that I am bound, so far as it is in my power, to practise what I pray for. And though I do not wish for the occasion every day, yet let me tell you, I would not willingly pass one day of my life without comforting a sad soul or showing mercy; and I praise God for this occasion. And now let's tune our instruments."

William Law

Old part of the Hall Yard House (now Hall Farm)
showing William Law's study window on left (see p.167)

WILLIAM LAW

William Law's spiritual teaching, while displaying the imprint of those who preceded him in the Christian mystical tradition, reflects the influence of several seventeenth-century revolutions and was addressed to the modern individuals they produced. The Glorious Revolution, bringing William and Mary to the throne in 1689, purged the monarchy of the Catholic inclinations characteristic of the Restoration era, a cleansing whose roots, of course, reach back into the long-standing efforts of the Puritans and the mid-century events surrounding the English Civil War. The Scientific Revolution was reaching its culmination in Isaac Newton's *Principia*, published the year after Law's birth, and the Enlightenment was building up steam and breathing new confidence into the authority of human reason, thus fuelling an increasing optimism for the ordered progress and perfectibility of human life.

The effects of these historic transformations gradually worked their way into every corner of English society, even into the village of King's Cliffe, in Northamptonshire, where Law was born in 1686. He apparently had a happy childhood as the son of a gentleman grocer and the brother of seven siblings, though a biographer suggests that there was "an intellectual as well as an emotional constriction in his upbringing," which included much Anglican instruction in the Bible and the Book of Common Prayer.[1]

The seriousness and religious strictness that characterized Law's approach to life are perhaps first evident in the set of eighteen "Rules for My Future Conduct," which emphasize judging all things by the "infallible Word of God," the fruitful use of time, and the observance of five-times-daily prayer, that he wrote down before leaving for Emmanuel College, Cambridge, in 1705. He graduated in 1708, became a Fellow of Emmanuel and was ordained a deacon in 1711, and received his M.A. in 1712. Following George I's accession to the throne in 1714, Law, unwilling to break his oath of allegiance to the Stuarts, whom he believed to be, by divine right, England's legitimate rulers, relinquished his Fellowship in 1716. In doing so, he declared himself a Non-juror and sacrificed his opportunities for official clerical or academic positions.

By 1727, probably after passing through a financially rocky period, Law had become a private tutor and chaplain to Edward Gibbon's son, who later became the father of the famous historian. Law took up residence in the pleasant and spacious Gibbon house at Putney, near (and now in) London, and for ten years lived as almost a member of the family, writing and teaching, through both word and deed, having been made a priest in the Non-juring Church in 1727.

Law returned to King's Cliffe in 1740 in order to set up a semi-monastic household near the parish church, somewhat similar to the community of Little Gidding founded by Nicholas Ferrar over a century earlier. He was joined there in 1744 by Hester Gibbon, the sister of his former pupil, and a wealthy widow named Elizabeth Hutcheson. The three of them, with Law as chaplain and spiritual director, lived a simple life of great devotion and almost boundless charity. Their combined financial resources were quite substantial, and they used most of it, except the tenth they kept for living expenses, to establish schools, a public library, and almshouses, and to support other charitable undertakings. Their beneficence was so great that the parish of King's Cliffe became known as something of a haven for paupers.

Law died at eight o'clock on the morning of 9 April 1761, at the age of seventy-five. Mrs Hutcheson passed away in 1781 and Hester Gibbon in 1790. All three participants in the experiment in holy living at King's Cliffe are buried in the cemetery of the parish church there.

The world Law left behind was one in which Enlightenment thinking was becoming firmly rooted. There was a general aversion to religious enthusiasm and the order of the day among most rational and respectable Anglicans was an easy-going, nominal

Christianity in which the demands of faith found a convenient compromise with the desires of society. Law was unwilling to tolerate such lukewarmness and in order to encourage his fellow Christians to join him on the straight and narrow path he wrote *A Serious Call to a Devout and Holy Life* in 1728. This is by far his most famous work, and of all English books of spiritual direction published after the Reformation is probably second only to *Pilgrim's Progress* in the degree of influence it has exercised. It inspired John Wesley and contributed to the Evangelical Revival in England, and its rigorous temper reveals Law's resemblance to Jonathan Edwards, his American contemporary who was contributing to a similar revival in New England.

Law's *Serious Call* is a plainly stated, elegantly written, and forceful summons to genuine devotion and against concessions to the ways of the world. Much of his other writing prior to his move to King's Cliffe consisted of brilliantly-argued attacks on the apparent moral laxity or theological unorthodoxy of other authors, including deists such as Matthew Tindal, who proposed that the validity of Christianity rests on reason not revelation. Law's refutation of deism pointed to the limitations of human reason in the realm of religious truth. But he perhaps took this message sincerely to heart only a few years later, when he realized that what was most needed for the true and effective spirituality he advocated was not argumentation but a deeper vision and transformation.

Law had long been familiar with the rich tradition of Christian mysticism extending from antiquity to his own time, but his thinking and writing did not take on a truly mystical tone until he became acquainted with, and deeply affected by, the seventeenth-century works of Jacob Boehme, the German shoemaker and philosopher. The books Law wrote at King's Cliffe, most notably *The Spirit of Prayer* and *The Spirit of Love*, in which he attempts to elucidate the farther reaches of Christian spirituality, reflect the profound influence of Boehme on his later work.

Boehme's writings seem to have provided Law with a framework within which he could deepen and expand his picture of the spiritual life, though the rather difficult and unusual ideas of this

Evangelical Lutheran mystic at first put Law into "a perfect sweat." But he soon came to revere Boehme as an "illuminated instrument of God" to whom were revealed the mysteries of creation, the fall, and the gradual redemption and reunification of the human and natural world. Law seized upon this system, this cosmic story, as a revelation of the full dimensions of the "devout and holy life" to which he was calling people. In *The Spirit of Prayer* (Part 1, ch. 2) he pointed out that the path of this sacred reunification leads inward, saying that "though God be everywhere present, yet he is only present to you in the deepest and most central part of your soul."[2]

Law shared with Boehme a love of the Bible and a disdain for bibliolatry—emphasizing the distinction between the written word and the cosmic Word—and a recognition of the superiority of intuitive over discursive reason in discerning the things of the spirit, concluding that real knowledge involves "the communion of the knowing and the known." They also shared the conviction that the essence of salvation lies in the overcoming of egocentrism. In the final pages of Law's *Spirit of Love*, which is written in the form of meditative dialogues, a disciple asks his master how he can attain to holiness. The master says that "the one true way of dying to self is most simple and plain, it wants no arts or methods, no cells, monasteries, or pilgrimages; it is equally practicable to everybody; it is always at hand; it meets you in everything, it is free from all deceit, and is never without success. . . . It is the way of patience, meekness, humility, and resignation to God."[3]

But inasmuch as the dying to which Law refers is a process of detaching one's attention from the protected territory of the self and gradually being born to the more open and expansive dimensions of creation, it is, indeed, a pilgrimage. And though the pursuit of spiritual practices is often in danger of becoming an opportunity for self-assertion rather than self-transcendence, the methods Law had proposed in *A Serious Call*, and which had become such a natural part of his life in King's Cliffe, were surely helpful, necessary even if not sufficient, in preparing the way for the deeper insights of *The Spirit of Love*. The relationship of these two works, the progression from the first to the second, is rather similar to the path depicted in Herbert's *The Temple*, where early moral precepts give way eventually to more purely spiritual inquiries.

The house occupied by Law, Gibbon, and Hutcheson is called the Hall Yard House and is located immediately east of King's Cliffe parish church. The house had also been known as King John's House and in the thirteenth century was possibly used as a lodge by both King John and his son Henry when they visited nearby Rockingham Forest, a Royal hunting ground.

Although there is no evidence that Law heard heavenly music as did Richard Rolle and Margery Kempe, he apparently enjoyed, as did George Herbert, the more mundane form performed by human hands and he occasionally hosted musical gatherings in the house, with Hester Gibbon playing the organ. The portion of the house to the left of the front door contained the trio's dining room on the ground floor and, upstairs, what was Gibbon's bedroom. Elizabeth Hutcheson's bedroom was at the back of the house, as were the breakfast room and kitchen, above which was Law's bedroom. Opening off from Law's bedroom, which, because of its location over the kitchen was probably the warmest room in the house, was his tiny study, only about five feet long and four feet wide. From the window in the study Law is supposed to have interviewed applicants for charity as they pled their cases from the ground below. Looking out of this window, Law could see, across the garden and a stream, the schools, library, and almshouses that he and his beneficent companions had founded and maintained, and which he visited regularly.

Life in the Hall Yard House followed an ascetic routine designed to deepen devotion and to facilitate charity, implementing the principles of *A Serious Call*, which, according to Law, can fill "our lives with the greatest peace and happiness that can be enjoyed in this world" (ch. 11). Law rose at five each morning and, after a time of private devotion, would have breakfast—a cup of chocolate—in his bedroom. Study and charitable works would occupy him until nine o'clock, at which time he would meet with the women for corporate prayer and devotion. He would then spend the remainder of the morning reading and writing.

We can imagine Law in his study, with the morning light spreading across the pages of the Bible and the works of Jacob Boehme, seeking to make himself transparent to the light that had illumined that German cobbler. Law believed that the influential ideas of Isaac Newton had also helped reveal the cosmic, even mystical, dimensions of light. In the writing Law undertook in this house, he explored these dimensions and sought an inner light beyond the light of reason, which he thought, perhaps excessively so, had become so blinding in his day.

The threesome would reassemble for the midday meal at noon in winter and at one o'clock in summer, with devotions afterward. Law would then study until joining the women for afternoon tea and "cheerful conversation," before another period of devotion and Bible reading. A refreshing walk outdoors would follow. The regular evening activities included a snack and final daily prayers, with the house retiring at nine o'clock. In addition to this daily routine would be visits from friends and family members, which sometimes involved playing with the children of Law's nephew, horseback and carriage rides through the countryside, and various community events.

The primary public activity of Law and the women was attending the services at the church, although, because of his Non-juror status, Law could not play any official role. His pew was immediately beneath the tower, which is the oldest part of the building, dating to the eleventh or twelfth century. There is also some evidence that an even more ancient Saxon building once occupied this site.

The original Norman tower had four round-arched windows, with Saxon-style central shafts, just above the ridge line of the nave. Only two of these windows, on the north and south sides, are now visible from the outside, the others having been blocked by later construction, but all four can be seen on the inside. The upper part of the spire, forming the belfry, was added in the thirteenth century.

The chancel still contains evidence of its thirteenth-century foundations at the base of the south wall, when it was built to replace the Norman church. But most of it dates from the major rebuilding undertaken in the fifteenth century, when a diagonal through-passage to the north transept was also added. On the north wall of the chancel is a memorial inscription to Law's father, Thomas. William Law himself was memorialized in 1891 when an anonymous woman gave an altar cross inscribed in his memory to be placed above the communion table.

The nave and flanking aisles are primarily fifteenth century, although remnants of the thirteenth century are still to be found in the west wall of the nave. On the outside of this wall, in the stonework surrounding the window, can be seen the lines of the smaller, steeper thirteenth-century structure.

Two fifteenth-century porches extend into the churchyard, the south one without windows, the north one with windows, benches, and a message for pilgrims. William Law's tomb is on the northeast side of the church. It is reminiscent of a writing desk and is inscribed at length with references to his achievements and qualities, saying in part, "in his last years he was wholly swallowed up in his love to God and mankind, so that Virtue in him was nothing else but Heavenly love and Heavenly flame." Indeed, on the day before he died in his room across the road, Hester Gibbon recorded him saying that "he had such an opening of the divine life within him, that the fire of divine love quite consumed him."[4] She is buried in the same vault as Law; Elizabeth Hutcheson in a separate tomb to the side.

The church is located on the north side of King's Cliffe, which by the late eleventh century was already a Royal Manor. The house in which Law was born lies along the main street, but it has been extensively altered since his time. In Bridge Street are Law's library and the school he founded, though the latter is in a state of disuse. The almshouses, still actively used, remain in good condition and there is still a Law and Hutcheson Charity that provides financial assistance to the needy. Situated about thirteen miles west of Peterborough off the A47, King's Cliffe is, incidentally, about the same distance north-west of the ecumenical community of Little Gidding.

Notes

1. A. Keith Walker, *William Law: His Life and Thought* (London: SPCK, 1973), p. 6. This is the best general account of Law's life, and much of the information for this introduction was derived from it.

2. William Law, *The Spirit of Prayer*, in vol. 7 of the *Works of the Reverend William Law* (London, 1762; reprint, Brockenhurst, Hants. and Canterbury, Kent: G. B. Morgan: 1892-3), p. 28. The extracts that follow are taken from this reprint. Stylistic conventions of capitalization, etc., have been modernized.

3. Law, *The Spirit of Love*, in vol. 8 of *Works*, p. 122.

4. Walker, *William Law*, p. 229.

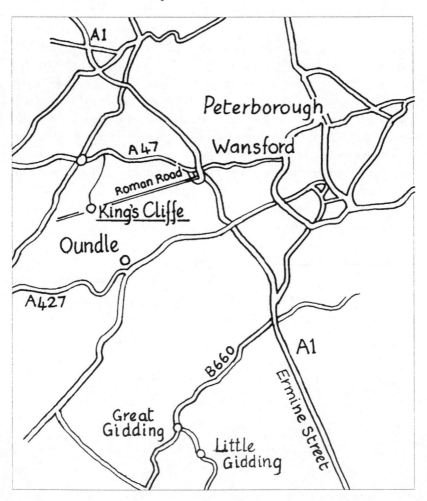

A SERIOUS CALL TO A DEVOUT AND HOLY LIFE

CHAPTER 11

Showing how great devotion fills our lives with the greatest peace and happiness that can be enjoyed in this world

Some people will perhaps object that all these rules of holy living unto God in all that we do are too great a restraint upon human life; that it will be made too anxious a state, by thus introducing a regard to God in all our actions. And that by depriving ourselves of so many seemingly innocent pleasures, we shall render our lives dull, uneasy and melancholy. To which it may be answered:

First: That these rules are prescribed for, and will certainly procure, a quite contrary end. That instead of making our lives dull and melancholy, they will render them full of content and strong satisfactions. That by these rules, we only change the childish satisfactions of our vain and sickly passions for the solid enjoyments and real happiness of a sound mind.

Second: That as there is no foundation for comfort in the enjoyments of this life but in the assurance that a wise and good God governs the world, so the more we find out God in everything, the more we apply to him in every place, the more we look up to him in all our actions, the more we conform to his will, the more we act according to his wisdom, and imitate his goodness, by so much the more do we enjoy God, partake of the divine nature, and heighten and increase all that is happy and comfortable in human life.

Third: He that is endeavouring to subdue and root out of his mind all those passions of pride, envy, and ambition that religion opposes, is doing more to make himself happy, even in this life, than he that is contriving means to indulge them. For these passions are the causes of all the disquiets and vexations of human life: they are the dropsies and fevers of our minds, vexing them with false appetites, and restless cravings after such things as we do not want, and spoiling our taste for those things which are our proper good.

Showing how difficult the practice of humility is made by the general spirit and temper of the world; how Christianity requires us to live contrary to the world

Every person, when he first applies himself to the exercise of this virtue of humility, must . . . consider himself as a learner, that is to learn something that is contrary to former tempers and habits of mind, and which can only be got by daily and constant practice.

He has not only as much to do as he that has some new art or science to learn, but he has also a great deal to unlearn: he is to forget and lay aside his own spirit, which has been a long while fixing and forming itself; he must forget and depart from abundance of passions and opinions, which the fashion and vogue and spirit of the world have made natural to him.

He must lay aside his own spirit, because as we are born in sin, so in pride, which is as natural to us as self-love, and continually springs from it. And this is the reason why Christianity is so often represented as a new birth and a new spirit.

He must lay aside the opinions and passions which he has received from the world, because the vogue and fashion of the world, by which we have been carried away, as in a torrent, before we could pass right judgments of the value of things, is, in many respects, contrary to humility: so that we must unlearn what the spirit of the world has taught us before we can be governed by the spirit of humility.

The Devil is called in Scripture the prince of this world, because he has great power in it, because many of its rules and principles are invented by this evil spirit, the father of all lies and falsehood, to separate us from God and prevent our return to happiness.

Now according to the spirit and vogue of this world, whose corrupt air we have all breathed, there are many things that pass for great and honourable and most desirable, which yet are so far from being so that the true greatness and honour of our nature consist in the not desiring them.

To abound in wealth, to have fine houses and rich clothes, to be beautiful in our persons, to have titles of dignity, to be above our fellow-creatures, to command the bows and obeisance of other people, to be looked on with admiration, to overcome our enemies with power, to set out ourselves in as much splendour as we can, to live highly and magnificently, to eat and drink and delight ourselves in the most costly manner—these are the great, the honourable, the desirable things to which the spirit of the world turns the eyes of all people. And many a man is afraid of standing still and not engaging in the pursuit of these things, lest the same world should take him for a fool.

The history of the gospel is chiefly the history of Christ's conquest over this spirit of the world. And the number of true Christians is only the number of those who, following the spirit of Christ, have lived contrary to this spirit of the world.

. . . .

You can make no stand against the assaults of pride, the meek affections of humility can have no place in your soul, till you stop the power of the world over you and resolve against a blind obedience to its laws.

And when you are once advanced thus far as to be able to stand still in the torrent of worldly fashions and opinions, and examine the worth and value of things which are most admired and valued in the world, you have gone a great way in the gaining of your freedom, and have laid a good foundation for the amendment of your heart.

For as great as the power of the world is, it is all built upon a blind obedience, and we need only open our eyes to get rid of its power.

THE SPIRIT OF PRAYER

Chapter 1

Treating of some matters preparatory to the spirit of prayer

The greatest part of mankind, nay of Christians, may be said to be asleep, and that particular way of life, which takes up each man's mind, thoughts, and actions, may be very well called his particular dream. This degree of vanity is equally visible in every form and order of life. The learned and the ignorant, the rich and the poor, are all in the same state of slumber, only passing away a short life in a different kind of dream. But why so? It is because man has an eternity within him, is born into this world not for the sake of living here, not for anything this world can give him, but only to have time and place, to become either an eternal partaker of a divine life with God, or to have a hellish eternity among fallen angels. And, therefore, every man who has not his eye, his heart, and his hands continually governed by this twofold eternity may be justly said to be fast asleep, to have no awakened sensibility of himself. And a life devoted to the interests and enjoyments of this world, spent and wasted in the slavery of earthly desires, may truly be called a dream, as having all the shortness, vanity, and delusion of a dream, only with this great difference: that when a dream is over, nothing is lost but fictions and fancies; but when the dream of life is ended *only* by death, all that eternity is lost for which we were brought into being.

Now there is no misery in this world, nothing that makes either the life or death of man to be full of calamity, but this blindness and insensibility of his state, into which he so willingly, nay obstinately, plunges himself. Everything that has the nature of evil and distress in it takes its rise from hence. Do but suppose a man to know himself, that he comes into this world on no other errand but to rise out of the vanity of time into the riches of eternity; do but suppose him to govern his inward thoughts and outward actions by this view of himself, and then to him every day has lost its evil: prosperity and adversity have no difference, because he receives and uses them both in the same spirit; life and death are equally welcome, because equally parts of his way to eternity. For poor and miserable as this life is, we have all of us free access to all that is great and good and happy, and carry within ourselves a key to all the treasures that heaven has to bestow upon us. We starve in the midst of plenty, groan under infirmities, with the remedy in our own hand, live and die without knowing and feeling anything of the one, only good, whilst we have it in our power to know and enjoy it in as great a reality as we know and feel the power of the world over us: for heaven is as near to our souls as this world is to our bodies, and we are created, we are redeemed, to have our conversation in it.

God, the only good of all intelligent natures, is not an absent or distant God, but is more present in and to our souls than our own bodies, and we are strangers to heaven, and without God in the world, for only this reason: because we are void of that spirit of prayer which alone can, and never fails to, unite us with the one, only good, and to open heaven and the kingdom of God within us. A root set in the finest soil, in the best climate, and blessed with all that sun and air and rain can do for it, is not in so sure a way of its growth to perfection as every man may be whose spirit aspires after all that which God is ready and infinitely desirous to give him. For the sun meets not the springing bud that stretches towards him with half that certainty as God, the source of all good, communicates himself to the soul that longs to partake of him.

. . . .

CHAPTER 2

Discovering the true way of turning to God and of finding the kingdom of heaven, the riches of eternity in our souls

You have seen, dear reader, the nature and necessity of regeneration: be persuaded, therefore, fully to believe, and firmly to settle in your mind this most certain truth, that all our salvation consists in the manifestation of the nature, life, and spirit of Jesus Christ, in our inward new man. This alone is Christian redemption; this alone delivers from the guilt and power of sin; this alone redeems, renews, and regains the first life of God in the soul of man. Everything besides this is self, is fiction, is propriety, is own will, and, however coloured, is only your old man, with all his deeds.

Enter therefore with all your heart into this truth, let your eye be always upon it, do everything in view of it, try everything by the truth of it, love nothing but for the sake of it. Wherever you go, whatever you do, at home or abroad, in the field or at church, do all in a desire of union with Christ, in imitation of his tempers and inclinations, and look upon all as nothing, but that which exercises and increases the spirit and life of Christ in your soul. From morning to night keep Jesus in your heart, long for nothing, desire nothing, hope for nothing, but to have all that is within you changed into the spirit and temper of the holy Jesus. Let this be your Christianity, your Church and your religion. For this new birth in Christ, thus firmly believed and continually desired, will do everything that you want to have done in you: it will dry up all the springs of vice, stop all the workings of evil in your nature; it will bring all that is good into you; it will open all the gospel within you, and you will know what it is to be taught by God.

This longing desire of your heart to be one with Christ will soon put a stop to all the vanity of your life, and nothing will be permitted to enter into your heart, or proceed from it, but what comes from God and returns to God: you will soon be as it were tied and bound in the chains of all holy affections and desires, your mouth will have a watch set upon it, your ears would willingly hear nothing that does not tend to God, nor your eyes be open but to see and find occasions of doing good. In a word, when this faith has got both your head and your heart, it will then be with you as it was with the merchant who found a pearl of great price; it will make you gladly to sell all that you have, and buy it. For all that had seized and possessed the heart of any man, whatever the merchant of this world had got together, whether of riches, power, honour, learning, or reputation, loses all its value, is counted but as dung, and willingly parted with, as soon as this glorious pearl, the new birth in Christ Jesus, is discovered and found by him.

This, therefore, may serve as a touchstone, whereby everyone may try the truth of his state: if the old man is still a merchant within you, trading in all sorts of worldly honour, power, or learning, if the wisdom of this world is not foolishness to you, if earthly interests and sensual pleasures are still the desire of your heart, and only covered under a form of godliness, a cloak of creeds, observances, and institutions of religion, you may be assured that the pearl of great price is not yet found by you. For where Christ is born, or his spirit rises up in the soul, there all self is denied and obliged to turn out; there all carnal wisdom, arts of advancement, with every pride and glory of this life, are as so many heathen idols all willingly renounced, and the man is not only content, but rejoices to say that his kingdom is not of this world.

But you will perhaps say: "How shall this great work, the birth of Christ, be effected in me?" It might rather be said: "Since Christ has an infinite power, and also an infinite desire, to save mankind, how can anyone miss of this salvation, but through his own unwillingness to be saved by him?" Consider: How was it that the lame and the blind, the lunatic and leper, the publican and sinner, found Christ to be their saviour, and to do all that for them that they wanted to be done to them? It was because they had a real desire of having that which they asked for, and therefore in true faith and prayer applied to Christ, that his spirit and power might enter into them and heal that which they wanted and desired to be healed in them. Every one of these said in faith and desire, "Lord, if you will, you can make me whole." And the answer was always this: "According to your faith, so be it done unto you." This is Christ's answer now, and thus it is done to every one of us at this day: as our faith is, so is it done unto us. And here lies the whole reason of our falling short of the salvation of Christ: it is because we have no will to it.

But you will say: "Do not all Christians desire to have Christ to be their saviour?" Yes, but here is the deceit: all would have Christ to be their saviour in the next world, and to help them into heaven when they die, by his power and merits with God. But this is not willing Christ to be your saviour, for his salvation, if it is had, must be had in this world; if he saves you, it must be done in this life, by changing and altering all that is within you, by helping you to a new heart, as he helped the blind to see, the lame to walk, and the dumb to speak. For to have salvation from Christ is nothing else but to be made like unto him; it is to have his humility and meekness, his mortification and self-denial, his renunciation of the spirit, wisdom, and honour of this world, his love of God, his desire of doing God's will, and seeking only his honour. To have these tempers formed and begotten in your heart is to have salvation from Christ. But if you will not to have these tempers brought forth in you, if your faith and desire do not seek and cry to Christ for them in the same reality as the lame asked to walk and the blind to see, then you must be said to be unwilling to have Christ be your saviour.

Again, consider: How was it that the carnal Jew, the deep-read scribe, the learned rabbi, the religious Pharisee, not only did not receive, but crucified their saviour? It was because they willed and desired no such saviour as he was, no such inward salvation as he offered to them. They desired no change of their own nature, no inward destruction of their own natural tempers, no deliverance from the love of themselves and the enjoyments of their passions; they liked their state, the gratification of their old man, their long robes, their broad phylacteries, and greetings in the market. They wanted not to have their pride and self-love dethroned, their covetousness and sensuality to be dethroned by a new nature from heaven derived into them. Their only desire was the success of Judaism, to have an outward saviour, a temporal prince, who would establish their law and ceremonies over all the earth. And therefore they crucified their dear redeemer and would have none of his salvation, because it all consisted in a change of their nature, in a new birth from above, and a kingdom of heaven to be opened within them by the Spirit of God.

Oh Christendom, look not only at the old Jews, but see yourself in this glass! For at this day (Oh sad truth to be told!), at this day, a Christ within us, an inward saviour raising a birth of his own nature, life and spirit within us, is rejected as gross enthusiasm; the learned rabbis take counsel against it. The propagation of Popery, the propagation of Protestantism, the success of some particular church, is the salvation which priests and people are chiefly concerned about.

But to return: It is manifest that no one can fail of the benefit of Christ's salvation, but through an unwillingness to have it, and from the same spirit and tempers as made the Jews unwilling to receive it. But if you would still further know how this great work, the birth of Christ, is to be effected in you, then let this joyful truth be told you: that this great work is already begun in every one of us. For this holy Jesus, who is to be formed in you, who is to be the saviour and new life of your soul, who is to raise you out of the darkness of death into the light of life, and give you power to become a son of God, is already within you, living, stirring, calling, knocking at the door of your heart, and wanting nothing but your own faith and good will to have as real a birth and form in you as he had in the Virgin Mary. For the eternal Word, or Son of God, did not then first begin to be the saviour of the world when he was born in Bethlehem of Judea, but that Word which became man in the Virgin Mary did, from the beginning of the world, enter as a word of life, a seed of salvation, into the first father of mankind, was inspoken into him, as an ingrafted word, under the name and character of a "bruiser of the serpent's head."

Hence it is that Christ said to his disciples, "the kingdom of God is within you"; that is, the divine nature is within you, given unto your first father, into the light of his life, and, from him, rising up in the life of every son of Adam. Hence also the holy Jesus is said to be "the light that lightens everyone who comes into the world." Not as he was born at Bethlehem, not as he had a human form upon earth—in these respects he could not be said to be the light of everyone who comes into the world—but as he was that eternal Word by which all things were created, which was the light and life of all things, and which had as a second creator entered again into fallen man, as a bruiser of the serpent: in this respect it was truly said of our Lord, when on earth, that he was "the light that lightens everyone who comes into the world."

For he was really and truly all this, as he was the Immanuel, the God-with-us, given unto Adam, and in him to all his offspring. See here the beginning and glorious extent of the Catholic Church of Christ: it takes in all the world; it is God's unlimited, universal mercy to all mankind; every human creature, as sure as he is born of Adam, has a birth of the bruiser of the serpent in him, and so is infallibly in covenant with God through Jesus Christ. Hence also it is that the holy Jesus is appointed to be judge of all the world: it is because all mankind, all nations and languages have in him, and through him, been put into covenant with God and made capable of resisting the evil of their fallen nature.

When our blessed Lord conversed with the woman at Jacob's well, he said to her: "If you knew the gift of God and who it is that is talking with you, you would have asked him and he would have given you living water." How happy, may anyone well say, was this woman of Samaria, to stand so near this gift of God, from whom she might have had living water, had she but vouchsafed to have asked for it! But, dear Christian, this happiness is yours, for this holy Jesus, the gift of God first given to Adam, and in him to all who are descended from him, is the gift of God to you, as sure as you are born of Adam: nay, had you never yet owned him, be you wandered from him, yet is he still with you, he is the gift of God to you, and if you will turn to him and ask of him, he has the living water for you.

Poor sinner, consider the treasure you have within you: the saviour of the world, the eternal Word of God lies hidden in you, as a spark of the divine nature, which is to overcome sin and death and hell within you, and generate the life of heaven again in your soul. Turn to your heart and your heart will find its saviour, its God, within itself. You see, hear, and feel nothing of God because you seek for him abroad with your outward eyes; you seek him in books, in controversies, in the Church and outward exercises, but there you will not find him, till you have first found him in your heart. Seek for him in your heart and you will never seek in vain, for there he dwells, there is the seat of his light and holy spirit.

For this turning to the light and spirit of God within you is your only true turning to God: there is no other way of finding him, but in that place where he dwells in you. For though God be everywhere present, yet he is only present to you in the deepest and most central part of your soul. Your natural senses cannot possess God, or unite you to him; nay, your inward faculties of understanding, will, and memory can only reach after God, but cannot be the place of his habitation in you. But there is a root or depth in you, from whence all these faculties come forth, as lines from a centre, or as branches from the body of a tree. This depth is called the centre, the fund, or bottom of the soul. This depth is the unity—the eternity, I had almost said—the infinity of your soul, for it is so infinite that nothing can satisfy it, or give it any rest, but the infinity of God. In this depth of the soul, the holy Trinity brought forth its own living image in the first created man, bearing in himself a living representation of Father, Son and Holy Ghost, and this was his dwelling in God and God in him. This was the kingdom of God within him, and made paradise without him. But the day that Adam did eat of the forbidden earthly tree, on that day he absolutely died to this kingdom of God within him. This depth or centre of his soul, having lost its God, was shut up in death and darkness, and became a prisoner in an earthly animal, which only excelled its brethren, the beasts, in an upright form and serpentine subtilty. Thus ended the Fall of Man. But from that moment that the God of mercy inspoke into Adam the bruiser of the serpent, from that moment all the riches and treasures of the divine nature came again into man, as a seed of salvation sown into the centre of his soul, and only lies hidden there in every man, till he desire to rise from his fallen state and to be born again from above.

Awake then, you that sleep, and Christ, who from all eternity has been espoused to your soul, shall give you light. Begin to search and dig in your own field for this pearl of eternity that lies hidden in it; it cannot cost you too much, nor can you buy it too dear, for it is all, and when you have found it, you will know that all you have sold or given away for it is as mere a nothing as a bubble upon the water.

Theophilus: But to explain this matter somewhat deeper to you, according to the mystery of all things opened by God in his chosen instrument, Jacob Boehme:

You know we have often spoken of eternal nature, that so sure as there is an eternal God, so sure is it that there is an eternal nature, as universal, as unlimited, as God himself, and everywhere working where God is, and therefore equally existent, as being his kingdom of heaven, or outward manifestation of the invisible riches, powers, and glories of the Deity.

Before, or without, nature, the Deity is an entire hidden, shut up, unknown and unknowable abyss. For nature is the only ground, or beginning, of something; there is neither this nor that, no ground for conception, no possibility of distinction or difference, there cannot be a creature to think, nor anything to be thought of, till nature is in existence. For all the properties of sensibility and sensible life, every mode and manner of existence, all seeing, hearing, tasting, smelling, feeling, all inclinations, passions, and sensations of joy, sorrow, pain, pleasure, etc., are not in God, but in nature. And, therefore, God is not knowable, not a thought can begin about him, till he manifests himself in, and through, and by the existence of nature: that is, till there is something that can be seen, understood, distinguished, felt, etc.

And this is eternal nature, the out-birth of the Deity, called the kingdom of heaven, *viz.*, an infinity, or boundless opening of the properties, powers, wonders, and glories of the hidden Deity, and this not once done, but ever doing, ever standing in the same birth, for ever and ever breaking forth and springing up in new forms and openings of the abyssal Deity, in the powers of nature. And out of this ocean of manifested powers of nature, the will of the Deity created hosts of heavenly beings, full of the heavenly wonders introduced into a participation of the infinity of God, to live in an eternal succession of heavenly sensations, to see and feel, to taste and find new forms of delight in an inexhaustible source of ever-changing and never-ceasing wonders of the divine glory.

Oh Theogenes! What an eternity is this, out of which, and for

182

which, your eternal soul was created? What little crawling things are all that an earthly ambition can set before you? Bear with patience for a while the rags of your earthly nature, the veil and darkness of flesh and blood, as the lot of your inheritance from Father Adam, but think nothing worth a thought but that which will bring you back to your first glory, and land you safe in the region of eternity.

. . . .

Theogenes: Oh Theophilus, you quite surprise me by thus showing me, with so much certainty, how the powers of eternity work in the things of time. Nothing is done on earth but by the unchangeable workings of the same spiritual powers that work after the same manner both in heaven and in hell. I now sufficiently see how man stands in the midst of heaven and hell, under an absolute necessity of belonging wholly to the one or wholly to the other, as soon as this cover of materiality is taken off from him.

For matter is his only wall of partition between them; he is equally nigh to both of them, and as light and love make all the difference there is between heaven and hell, so nothing but a birth of light and love in the properties of his soul can possibly keep hell out of it, or bring heaven into it.

I now also see the full truth and certainty of what you said of the nature and power of divine love, *viz.*, that "it is perfect peace and joy, a freedom from all disquiet, making everything to rejoice in itself; that it is the Christ of God and wherever it comes, it comes as the blessing and happiness of every natural life, as the restorer of every lost perfection, a redeemer from all evil, a fulfiller of all righteousness, and a peace of God which passes all understanding." So that I am now a thousand times more than ever thirsty for the spirit of love. I am willing to sell all and buy it; its blessing is so great and the want of it so dreadful a state that I am even afraid of lying down in my bed till every working power of my soul is given up to it, wholly possessed and governed by it.

Theophilus: You have reason for all that you say, Theogenes, for were we truly affected with things, as though they were our real good or real evil, we should be much more afraid of having the serpents of covetousness, envy, pride, and wrath, well nourished and kept alive within us, than of being shut up in a pest-house, or cast into a dungeon of venomous beasts. On the other hand, we should look upon the lofty eloquence and proud virtue of a Cicero but as the blessing of storm or tempest, when compared with the heavenly tranquillity of that meek and lowly heart, to which our redeemer has called us.

I said the "serpents" of covetousness, envy, pride, and wrath, because they are alone the real, dreadful, original serpents, and all earthly serpents are but transitory, partial, and weak out-births of them. All evil earthly beasts are but short-lived images, or creaturely eruptions, of that hellish disorder that is broken out from the fallen spiritual world, and by their manifold variety they show us that multiplicity of evil that lies in the womb of that abyss of dark rage, which (*N.B.*) has no maker but the three first properties of nature, fallen from God and working in their own darkness.

. . . .

Theogenes: I could almost say that you have shown me enough of this monster of self, though I would not be without this knowledge of it for half the world. But now, Sir, what must I do to be saved from the mouth of this lion, for he is the depth of all subtlety, the Satan that deceives the whole world? He can hide himself under all forms of goodness, he can watch and fast, pray much and preach long, give alms to the poor, visit the sick, and yet often gets more strength and life, and a more immovable abode, in these forms of virtue than he has in publicans and sinners.

Enjoin me therefore whatever you please: all rules, methods, and practices will be welcome to me, if you judge them to be necessary in this matter.

Theophilus: There is no need of a number of practices or methods in this matter. For to die to self, or to come from under its power, is not, cannot be, done by any active resistance we can make to it by the powers of nature. For nature can no more overcome or suppress itself than wrath can heal wrath. So long as nature acts, nothing but natural works are brought forth, and therefore the more labour of this kind, the more nature is fed and strengthened with its own food.

But the one true way of dying to self is most simple and plain; it wants no arts or methods, no cells, monasteries or pilgrimages; it is equally practicable to everybody; it is always at hand; it meets you in everything, it is free from all deceit, and is never without success.

You may ask: "What is this one true, simple, plain, immediate, and unerring way?" It is the way of patience, meekness, humility, and resignation to God. This is the truth and perfection of dying to self; it is nowhere else, nor possible to be in anything else, but in this state of heart.

EPILOGUE
The Tradition Continues

The individuals represented in the preceding pages are, of course, merely some of the most significant figures along the way of the English mystical tradition. The road they travelled was peopled by innumerable other pilgrims and has been paralleled for centuries by seekers in other countries and religious traditions. Together they form a vital and venerable spiritual path, to which twentieth-century England has made some notable contributions. In the opening decades of the century Evelyn Underhill (1875-1941), who, in addition to being a poet, novelist, and writer on mysticism was also an influential spiritual counsellor, produced several important works. Her *Mysticism* (1911) has become one the classic introductions to the nature and development of mysticism, and she has written many other books with a more practical emphasis, including *Practical Mysticism* (1915) and *The Spiritual Life* (1937). A biography by C. J. R. Armstrong, entitled simply *Evelyn Underhill*, was published in 1975.

With Bede Griffiths (1906-93), the tradition of Western mysticism reached out to embrace that of the East. From the moment as a teenager when he apprehended a mysterious Presence in the sounds and forms of nature bathed in the evening light, he sought God in the solitude of the natural world and in intellectual pursuits at Oxford. But he found God, as he said in his autobiographical *The Golden String* (1954), "in the society of his Church and in the spirit of charity" (p. 17). Having become a Benedictine monk in 1933, he lived at Prinknash Abbey, Farnborough Abbey, and Pluscarden Priory in England until 1955. He then went to India to assist in founding a Christian community which would incorporate the customs of a Hindu monastery or ashram, and he lived there, at Saccidananda Ashram by the banks of the sacred river Cauvery, until his recent death. He wrote a number of books, dealing primarily with the integration of Eastern and Western spirituality, including *Return to the Centre* (1976), *The Marriage of East and West* (1982), and *A New Vision of Reality: Western Science, Eastern Mysticism, and Christian Faith* (1989). Kathryn Spink published a biography, *A Sense of the Sacred,* in 1988 and John Swindells has produced a biographical videotape called *A Human Search*, which is available from the Parabola Video Library in New York City. Audiotapes of dialogues with Griffiths are available from New Dimensions Foundation in San Francisco.

The modern Christian mystic that Bede Griffiths once identified as "the best spiritual guide in the Church today" is John Main (1926-82). In the Foreword to Main's *The Inner Christ* (1987), Griffiths said that Main "has recovered for Christians a way of prayer which links us with the earliest tradition of the Church and at the same time relates us to the most authentic tradition of prayer and meditation in other religions." Main was also a Benedictine monk, leaving a promising legal career in 1959 to pursue more deeply the path of meditative prayer. In his reading of *The Cloud of Unknowing* and the writings of John Cassian, he rediscovered the power of the mantra that he had first encountered during a sojourn in Malaya with the British Colonial Service many years earlier. His vision of the centrality of meditative prayer in the Christian life brought him eventually to Montreal, where, in 1977, he founded the Montreal Priory as a Christian meditation centre for both monks and lay people. His books, which provide a wealth of practical daily guidance and inspiration, include *The Joy of Being* (1987), *The Heart of Creation* (1988), and *The Way of Unknowing* (1989). A biography of Main, by Neil McKenty, is entitled *In the Stillness Dancing* (1986). Numerous audiotapes and videotapes of Main's talks can be obtained from the Christian Meditation Centre in Montreal, which also sponsors a variety of meditation programmes.

* * * * *

Finally, a passage from the Preface to Geraldine Hodgson's *English Mystics*, though addressed to an English audience in 1922, retains its relevance for all readers today and expresses the sentiment of the present author:

> If the book should serve to restore the idea of the mystical temper as a desirable possibility for sane and practical Englishmen, and to show that, in varying forms, it has been in every age not only a possibility but a fact, it may perhaps prove not wholly useless to a generation marked by a spirit of inquiry and unsatisfied desire.